The Dyscalculia Assessment

Jane Emerson and Patricia Babtie
Foreword by Brian Butterworth

continuum

A Companion Website to accompany this book is available online at:
http://education.emersonbabtie.continuumbooks.com
Please visit the link and register with us to receive your password and to access these downloadable resources.
If you experience any problems accessing the resources, please contact Continuum at:
info@continuumbooks.com

Continuum International Publishing Group

The Tower Building	80 Maiden Lane
11 York Road	Suite 704
London	New York
SE1 7NX	NY 10038

www.continuumbooks.com

British Library Cataloguing-in-Publication Data
A catalogue record for this book is available from the British Library.

ISBN: 9781441140852 (paperback)

Library of Congress Cataloging-in-Publication Data
Emerson, Jane.
The dyscalculia assessment / Jane Emerson and Patricia Babtie; foreword by Brian Butterworth.
    p. cm.
Includes bibliographical references.
    ISBN 978-1-4411-4085-2 (pbk.)
    1. Mathematics—Study and teaching. 2. Dyslexic children—Education. 3. Learning disabilities—Education. I. Babtie, Patricia. II. Title.

QA11.2.E45 2010   371.9'0447—dc22

Typeset by Pindar NZ, Auckland, New Zealand
Printed and bound in Great Britain by Bell&Bain Ltd, Glasgow

Contents

This book is dedicated to the memory of Dorian Yeo

Acknowledgements

Thank you to the late Dorian Yeo who pioneered a new approach to teaching numeracy at Emerson House inspired by the work of Steve Chinn and his colleagues at Mark College, to Kathryn Dickinson, Liz Barber and Ning Fulford for their contributions and to all the other teachers at Emerson House, both past and present, who have helped over the years. Generous support and encouragement has been given by Professor Brian Butterworth of University College London and Chris Messenger who set up the Harrow Dyscalculia Project, Dr Sue Gifford at Roehampton University and Professor Diana Laurillard at the London Knowledge Lab. SENCOs Sue Dillon and Angela King have made valuable practical suggestions. Andrew Walker has been patient and encouraging throughout this project. James Barry, Lucinda Barry, Karen Sosa and William, John and Ann Babtie have kindly read and commented on numerous drafts. Finally, thank you to Philippa Cook who modelled for the cover and to all the children who have taught us so much over the years.

Jane Emerson
Patricia Babtie

Foreword

In this important new book, Jane Emerson and Patricia Babtie lay out in a clear and systematic way how teachers can identify dyscalculic learners, and how they can help them achieve proficiency in basic arithmetic. Jane and Patricia are both very experienced special needs teachers whose recommendations are built on many years of teaching dyscalculic learners. Both of the authors, like me, have learnt a great deal about how best to do this from Dorian Yeo, perhaps the deepest thinker in the field of dyscalculia intervention.

One of the great strengths of *The Dyscalculia Assessment* is the way it shows the teacher how to identify in detail the strengths and weaknesses of each individual learner. This is fundamental to devising an individual learning plan that is crucial for the learner to make the best progress. *The Dyscalculia Assessment* explains how to analyse errors and what and how to teach, in order to overcome the difficulties. Teaching starts with concrete materials, such as counters, Base Ten materials, Stern Blocks and Cuisenaire Rods. The learner uses these to help them reason about the relationships between numbers, which enables them to become confident in tackling the arithmetical symbols that the rest of us find perfectly easy to understand. As with dyslexia, the key to success is making the right assessment, and using this to create the right plan for each learner.

Getting the assessment right is no easy matter. I developed a *Dyscalculia Screener* which was designed just to distinguish the dyscalculic learner from other low-attaining learners. But that's all my *Screener* does. To devise a learning plan tailored to each individual, the teacher needs to go beyond this, and this is what *The Dyscalculia Assessment* aims to do. There is a very useful Appendix that includes a commentary on the Wechsler Intelligence Scale for Children (WISC IV) and how to combine the information from educational psychologists' WISC reports with the specialized assessments suggested in the book.

One of the problems that many teachers and special educational needs coordinators (SENCOs), not to mention educational policy-makers, face is to distinguish dyscalculia from other reasons for poor maths performance. *The Dyscalculia Assessment* also outlines other co-occurring conditions such as dyslexia and dyspraxia that may cause difficulties in learning maths.

Developmental dyscalculia, like developmental dyslexia, is a condition the learner is born with that affects the ability to understand even very simple number concepts. Dyscalculic learners will struggle recognizing that the abstract digit 5 represents the concept that a collection of five will always be five however the collection is arranged. Learning basic arithmetical facts such as number bonds to ten can seem like learning to repeat sounds in an unknown language. We are beginning to understand how the brains of dyscalculic learners are different from typical learners, but we still do not know why they are different. Many cases of dyscalculia, like dyslexia, run in families, suggesting a genetic cause; however, many cases occur in mathematically typical families, suggesting that there may be other causes.

Many dyscalculic children remain dyscalculic into adulthood, but we do not yet know whether all do. Of course, the vast majority of these learners did not have the benefit of our modern understanding of the dyscalculic condition, and did not have the benefit of the specialized skilled intervention that is proposed here.

The Dyscalculia Assessment will be a valuable resource for special needs teachers helping dyscalculics. It will also be valuable for special educational needs coordinators who want to understand the special needs of dyscalculic learners. There is plenty of guidance, including a suggested script, so the assessment can be used by classroom teachers with no training in special needs. The detailed guidance on how to interpret the results, and what to teach in order to overcome the difficulties, provides the information needed to draw up practical provision maps and individual education plans (IEPs). It will be helpful for parents who want to understand why their child is doing so poorly in maths, while doing so well in other subjects, and how they can enjoy helping them using the games and activities.

Brian Butterworth
Professor of Cognitive Neuropsychology, University College London

Introduction: how to use the assessment

This book is for those wanting to investigate a child's numeracy levels in order to plan an intervention programme for individuals or small groups. It is aimed at teachers, teaching assistants and special educational needs coordinators.

There is an introduction to dyscalculia (Chapter 1) and the problems with numeracy (Chapter 2), and an overview of The Dyscalculia Assessment (Chapter 3). The main part of the book contains detailed instructions with a suggested script for conducting The Dyscalculia Assessment and forms for recording the findings (Chapter 4). The interpretation section explains how possible errors may arise and gives advice for formulating a teaching plan (Chapter 5). There are activities and games for multi-sensory teaching (Chapter 6).

The Appendices contain explanations of the Dyscalculia Screener and the Wechsler Intelligence Scale for Children (WISC IV), a sample report, a summary maths profile, group grid, questionnaire for teachers and parents, and a sample form for an individual teaching plan. There is also an appendix of resources including useful websites, equipment suppliers and useful organizations as well as templates for cards for the games. At the end of the book there is a glossary of terms and suggestions for further reading. Extra forms for recording the assessment can be downloaded from the Companion Website, http://education.emersonbabtie.continuumbooks.com.

The Dyscalculia Assessment

The Dyscalculia Assessment was devised at Emerson House in London to identify the specific numeracy problems a child has, rather than to diagnose a condition. Emerson House is a specialist centre in London supporting pupils with difficulties in numeracy and literacy.

The assessment is designed to be used with primary school children, whose intellectual level lies within the average range of intelligence, who are found to have significant maths learning difficulties. However, it could be used with older children.

The assessment is a detailed investigation into what the child can do and how they think about numeracy. It starts with an initial discussion about the child's attitudes to school and numeracy. There is a suggested script to provide guidance while investigating the pupil's knowledge and skills in number sense, counting and the number system, calculation, place value, multiplication and division, word problems, and formal written numeracy.

It can be done in one hour or over several sessions. It is not necessary to complete the whole assessment but only until enough information has been gained to formulate a teaching plan. The length of time required will depend on the speed and ability of the child. You should stop after the child has made two or three errors in a section and proceed to investigate the next section. If the child has significant difficulty with many of the early stages there is no point in continuing with the assessment; you will have already identified the point at which teaching must start, as well as the initial areas of concern.

The Dyscalculia Assessment is an informal diagnostic assessment. It aims to conduct the investigation in an atmosphere that is friendly and non-threatening in order to reduce any anxiety to the minimum possible. It provides information about why a child is not learning, or why they are underachieving. It provides detailed information about areas of strength and weakness in key areas of early maths development from which to develop a plan for a suitable approach to teaching.

The results give information about a particular child, without comparing them with their peers.

The evidence gathered is used to devise a detailed personalized plan for the child. Children at similar stages of numeracy development could be taught together.

Who is The Dyscalculia Assessment designed for?

The assessment is designed for primary school children within the average range of intelligence who are having difficulty learning maths. However, the assessment could be used for children above or below the average range in order to determine starting points for devising an individual teaching plan for them. It can also be used with older children who have significant maths weaknesses.

Who can carry out The Dyscalculia Assessment?

The assessment is informal and can be carried out by:
- maths teachers
- specialists trained and experienced in teaching children with special educational needs
- special educational needs coordinators (SENCOs)
- teaching assistants with some experience in working with children with low levels of numeracy.

Basic maths knowledge is required in order to be able to observe and identify the strengths and weaknesses of the child, such as memory or reasoning in maths learning. The assessor needs to make detailed notes of the child's attitude as well as their responses during the session. It could be helpful to video other colleagues carrying out an assessment so that a group of people involved with a child could discuss the findings and the implications for a teaching plan.

Do you need any other information to carry out the assessment?

The Dyscalculia Assessment can be used on its own. However, if any other co-occurring conditions are suspected, you will need more information about them. There are complex connections between specific learning difficulties, such as dyslexia, dyspraxia and attention deficit disorder, which impact on dyscalculia and are discussed on page 7.

Although the assessment can stand alone, it is helpful to collect information from parents, teachers and from any standardized tests which have been carried out. Information may be available from educational psychologists, as well as speech and language therapists, occupational therapists and physiotherapists. This information may include results from other subjects which will help to build a picture of how specific the problem is to maths or if it is affecting other aspects of the child's education.

How do you use the results to help your pupil?

Carefully analyse the child's responses which show evidence through errors or through lack of understanding or knowledge. Chapter 5 on interpretation gives examples of the common errors made by children struggling with maths. Use this information to draw up a teaching plan that directly addresses the child's difficulties. If the results are entered on a Group Grid (see page 166) it will be clear which children have similar mathematical needs so that they can be put into small groups for extra teaching.

Teaching suggestions and practical ways to move forward

Find the earliest point where knowledge or understanding has broken down. It is important to start from a baseline of success so teaching will begin from what the child can do and move forward from that point. It is essential to move slowly in very small steps without making assumptions about what is known or understood.

Children should use appropriate concrete materials to support their thinking and be encouraged to have a dialogue with the teacher to explain what they are doing. Make sure that children talk about what they are thinking while they are using the materials. Practical activities and specially devised maths games are effective ways of teaching specific concepts while encouraging children to reason.

Games are a particularly effective way of helping children to acquire confidence, knowledge and understanding. Some children quickly progress when the approach is appropriate to their needs. Others with more serious difficulties may make very slow progress. It is not possible to know how quickly a child will progress once given suitable help but often slow progress will indicate that the difficulty is severe. Children with significant numeracy difficulties learn best and develop some reasoning skills when a multi-sensory approach is used. The child should also be encouraged to talk about what they are thinking and doing through a positive discussion with their teacher. This can be called guided learning and needs to be delivered through a dialogue with the child.

What is dyscalculia?

Dyscalculia is an umbrella term used to refer to various conditions that cause specific difficulties with maths, such as developmental dyscalculia[1], mathematical disability, numerical learning disability, and number fact disorder among other terms. For the sake of clarity, we use the term 'dyscalculia' throughout the book to refer to different levels of difficulty with maths.

> Developmental dyscalculia is a condition that affects the ability to acquire arithmetical skills. Dyscalculic learners may have difficulty understanding simple number concepts, lack an intuitive grasp of numbers, and have problems learning number facts and procedures. Even if they produce a correct answer or use a correct method, they may do so mechanically and without confidence. (DfES 2001)

Numbers

Being numerate means understanding what a number is and how numbers relate to each other. Counting underpins basic numeracy. Dyscalculics may have difficulty learning to count and remembering which number follows another, especially the numbers between 10 and 20, with 13 to 19 often referred to as the 'teen' numbers. They may also persist in thinking of numbers as a random string of sounds or see them as varying 'clumps' of ones. They do not perceive patterns within numbers, such as two and two within four, or understand the relationships between numbers, for example that six is one more than five. They do not understand the place value system in which the value of a digit depends on its position in the number nor do they understand the principle of exchange which underpins place value.

Number facts

The basic number facts are all the number bonds of each of the numbers 1 to 10. For example, the number 5 can represent a quantity of five items or two quantities of four and one, or three and two, or two and three, or one and four depending on the way the five is looked at in terms of containing two components or parts. Dyscalculics have a unitary concept of each number and do not understand that numbers can be seen to be made of different combinations. These are widely known as number bonds. For example a bond of 5 is 3 plus 2.

Numerical operations

Numerical operations are the actions performed on numbers. The four operations are addition, subtraction, multiplication and division. Dyscalculics have difficulty understanding the concepts of these four operations. They are often unable to remember the procedures for carrying out calculations.

Place value and the principle of exchange

Early recording systems, such as tally marks, allotted one symbol to each item counted. In the place value system any quantity can be represented by using only ten digits (0 to 9). The value of the digit depends on its place in the number. Understanding this concept is difficult for many children. First they must understand the principle of exchange. This is the idea that several items can be exchanged for a different item which then represents the initial quantity. e.g. 10 one pence coins equal one 10p coin.

What causes dyscalculia?

At present there is very little agreement about what causes dyscalculia. Research into dyscalculia is at an early stage, but some researchers believe that it is caused by the way the brain is structured. Cognitive neuroscientists using brain imaging techniques suggest that these differences may be located in the parietal lobe (Dehaene 1997, Butterworth 1999). Significant maths difficulties may also be caused by other coexisting conditions, and this is discussed below.

Dyscalculia and other conditions

When dyscalculia coexists with other conditions such as dyslexia, dyspraxia, attention deficit disorder (ADD) and attention deficit hyperactivity disorder (ADHD) these are known as co-morbid or co-occurring conditions. Maths anxiety can result from having maths difficulties and can also exacerbate a maths difficulty. Some of the ways in which dyscalculia and co-occurring conditions affect maths learning are discussed on page 7.

How common is dyscalculia?

About 5 per cent of school-age children have dyscalculia. In 'Young children's difficulties in learning Mathematics', a review of the research, Sue Gifford says that although findings of prevalence studies ranged between 3 and 6 per cent, Shalev *et al.* (2000) 'concluded that a realistic estimate was 5%, as with dyslexia. Many current sources agree with this' (Gifford 2005). Researchers have found it difficult to establish how many people suffer from dyscalculia because different criteria are used for diagnosis (Wilson 2004).

Is there a cure?

Dyscalculia is not a disease so therefore there is no cure. Many dyscalculics can become competent mathematicians if they are taught appropriately using a structured, multi-sensory teaching approach such as that developed at Emerson House (Kay and Yeo 2003, Yeo 2003, Butterworth and Yeo 2004).

How do you identify and address dyscalculia?

At the time of writing the main method for finding objective evidence of dyscalculia is by using the Dyscalculia Screener devised by Brian Butterworth (2003). (See Appendix 1, page 156, for information on the Screener). This is a computer-based test that measures reaction times which are then compared with other measures that have been found by Professor Butterworth to be associated with the condition.

The Dyscalculia Assessment identifies the specific numeracy problems a child has, rather than diagnosing a condition. It investigates the child's knowledge and skills from the early stages of numeracy. It is essential to find the point at which they have failed to acquire some fact or concept that is crucial to numeracy development. Teaching should start at this point using a structured multi-sensory approach which uses real objects to explore maths ideas with the child discussing what they are doing.

Note

1. Developmental dyscalculia refers to a maths difficulty that a child is born with. This is to distinguish it from acquired dyscalculia, which is caused by accidental brain damage.

Numeracy, dyscalculia and co-occurring conditions

What does it mean to have a sense of number?

Maths provides an efficient way of making sense of the world, of explaining and representing the patterns and relationships in our world in a universally understandable form. The foundation of all maths skills is a sense of number. Number sense is the ability to understand what numbers represent and to use them to solve problems.

> The key components of number sense . . . include an awareness of numbers and their uses in the world around us, a good sense of place value concepts, approximation, estimation, and magnitude, the concept of numeration, and an understanding of comparisons and the equivalence of different representations and forms of numbers. (New Jersey Mathematics Coalition 1996)

The symbols 0 to 9 are combined in various ways to form all possible numbers. Understanding that these **abstract** symbols are derived and abstracted from a quantity of concrete objects is crucial to understanding numeracy. However, for some pupils the symbols 0 to 9 are meaningless, either because the symbols themselves have no meaning for them, or because they have no sense of the relationship between numbers. For example, they do not understand that five is one more than four, not merely the number that comes after four.

The sense about quantity, with which most infants are believed to be born, is often referred to as a sense of numerosity. This is part of what is called early **number sense** in the maths literature. In essence, it seems to be the sense that is strangely lacking in some people showing characteristics which lie under the umbrella term of dyscalculia.

Why is maths hard for some children?

Maths is:

- **abstract** in the sense that children may not relate the symbols to quantity
- a **building-block** subject where one fact leads to another: $2 + 2 = 4$ so $2 + 3 = 5$
- **complex**, with many ways of representing equivalents such as $3/6 = 1/2$.

When very early numeracy is taught in an **abstract** way using only mathematical symbols, without using concrete equipment, at a point too early in their development, many children will fail to grasp the crucial connection between real objects and abstract symbols. The numeracy aspect of maths should be based on working with actual quantities of objects and the visible relationships between them. Children need enough time to experience these relationships and connections. Some may need more time than others before moving forward. For example, children may be presented with the abstract question of $4 + 3 = ?$ It is less abstract to put the numbers in a context. 'If you have 4 sweets and then you get 3 more sweets, how many sweets do you have altogether?' It is more obvious to show pictures of sweets to demonstrate the question, but even a picture is only a two-dimensional representation of the concrete object. Some children, of all ages, may need to work with real objects that can be touched and moved and counted, especially when new concepts are taught. Those with specific difficulties such as poor concentration, or dyslexia and dyspraxia, will need to repeat these activities many times to gain consistent experiences that develop their own stable and reliable sense of quantity, which adds to their developing number sense.

Maths can be seen to develop like **building blocks** within topics. New concepts within each topic are developed from more basic concepts. If the earlier concepts are not fully understood, the pupil will not be able to make sense of the more advanced concepts. In addition, they must be able to reason from previously learnt facts which are stored in long-term memory.

Maths is **complex**. It involves concepts of time, quantity, space and the language of maths. Mastery of the four operations (addition, subtraction, multiplication and division) requires not only factual knowledge but also conceptual understanding and calculation proficiency as well as a memory of the procedures. Word problems also have to be solved by first understanding the words used and then by applying the right operation to them.

What do you need to learn maths?

Some of the main skills which underpin maths learning are:
- a sense of number
- long-term memory
- short-term memory
- working memory
- an ability to learn crucial sequences of words and numbers.

A sense of number or 'number sense' can then be described as an intuitive 'feel' for numbers, with added understanding that a certain number represents a specific quantity or value, and that it is part of a sequence and can be compared with other numbers. Number sense underlies the ability to make sense of number relationships, patterns within and between numbers, and the way numbers are built from other numbers.

Brian Butterworth (1999) has written extensively about 'infant numerosities' and described how very young children are aware of these quantitative differences and are able to distinguish differences in small numerosities from four or five months old. Numerosity is the 'perception of numerical quantities [that allows you] to compute their exact number' (Dehaene 1997). This is computed without counting the items one by one and is known as subitizing, which is the ability to take in the quantity of an array of objects at a glance and without counting. This is likely to be an aspect of paying attention to an array of objects coupled with looking at the quantity involved. It seems to rely on a certain level of this attention being paid by the child to very small quantities of objects made available in the child's environment. It is also taken to be an ability to recognize small numerosities: collections of up to four objects. The majority of people can enumerate up to four or five items without counting them one by one. It is easier to do this subitizing if objects are arranged in patterns, such as dice patterns. Dice patterns have been written about in the literature for many years as an important aid to pattern recognition. This assessment considers recognition of the dot patterns on the usual dice used for games, to be an important indicator of a child's developing number sense.

A good **long-term memory** is needed to retain facts and procedures over time. Long-term memory is the ability to store information, which can be retrieved again over a reasonably long period of time. In maths, certain essential facts, such as the bonds of ten, and fundamental procedures, such as column arithmetic, need to be stored for later use. If this information is not used at regular intervals it will gradually disappear.

The **short-term memory** is the memory required to recall things that are only needed temporarily, such as remembering a new telephone number for immediate use. Once the information has been used it can be forgotten without adverse effects.

Working memory is the memory needed to carry out step-by-step procedures and to reason. Working memory enables you to hold information in mind while performing other actions.

If a few basic facts are learnt off by heart, they can be used to derive other facts from the basics, by using the working memory, without children having to learn a large number of facts off by heart. For those with weak long-term memory skills the working memory can therefore be utilized instead, to reason from known facts to unknown ones. Conversely, those with poor working memories may have to try to learn more facts off by heart to reduce the demands on their weak working memory.

Sequences are groups of words that have a defined, regular relationship. Sequences of numbers are lists of numbers arranged according to a rule to create a pattern. If you know the rule that governs the relationship between them you can continue the pattern (Tapson 2006). For some sequences the order of items is an integral part of their full meaning such as the days of the week, the alphabet and, of course, counting.

Weaknesses in maths learning skills

Learning maths becomes difficult if there are weaknesses in a sense of number, in the various types of memory, and in sequencing.

A poor sense of number, or a weak intuitive grasp of numbers, leads to a ones-based number concept. Children with this problem tend to see each number as collections or 'piles' of ones. Often they will represent them using tally marks. This is sometimes described as not understanding the 'two-ness' of two. A weak sense of number causes poor understanding of number structures, with a lack of awareness that numbers contain other numbers. For example, 4 can mean 4 but also can be 'seen' as 2 and 2 or 3 and 1. This lack of awareness often leads to difficulties understanding many calculation methods and number concepts. Children with a poor sense of number tend to view almost every mathematical operation as an instruction to count or as a completely new problem. They cannot relate it to what has been previously learnt, or to a recent calculation that has been solved.

Long-term memory difficulties lead to difficulty remembering maths facts 'by heart'. Some pupils with maths difficulties have very poor long-term memory for verbally encoded facts (facts that are learnt, stored and remembered as verbal associations). If maths facts are presented to them only verbally, it may be meaningless to them unless the meaning is demonstrated and discussed using concrete objects.

Children with these memory weaknesses will be worse than most children at remembering maths procedures, such as long division, over time unless they are regularly revised.

Short-term memory problems can lead to children forgetting what the question was before they have even reached an answer. Very little learning is transferred into long-term memory without substantial over-learning involving extra practice and revision at regular intervals. These children need to learn to record their thinking on paper as they work.

Working memory difficulties: Typically, children with maths difficulties cannot easily select an appropriate strategy to solve a problem, nor can they usually remember or follow the steps of the procedures for working out calculations. They are often slow to work out an answer because they lose track of what they are doing while they are doing it. This weakness also affects their ability to learn number facts because they have forgotten the question they were working on and so receive fewer reminders of the answers to common questions concerning everyday number facts.

Sequencing difficulties affect many aspects of maths learning:

- following a series of instructions – first you . . . then you . . . and next you . . .
- processing and remembering the many different counting sequences, such as counting in twos or fives.
- managing the double sequential load of counting to calculate. For example, to work out 4 + 3 the child has difficulty counting and keeping track of how many steps have been counted. In order to count on 3 more, it is necessary to hold in mind the 3 counting steps while simultaneously subvocalizing or counting out loud from 4.

The Counting Trap

'The Counting Trap' was coined by Professor Eddie Gray (Thompson 1997). He wrote about the link between working memory difficulties, sequencing difficulties and persistent counting to work out facts which is the crucial factor that leads to chronic maths difficulties where little or no progress is made in spite of repeated revision. Each operation is seen as an instruction to count. The facts never become known automatically and the very counting becomes a 'trap'.

Counting

Counting is the activity that helps children to make sense of the spoken number system. Traditionally, it has been assumed that all children will become familiar with and will grow to understand the number system through counting. This turns out not necessarily to be the case. Some children need to be specifically shown how the number system is made out of repeated groups of tens. The savage irony is that you must be able to count but then you must be able to develop more sophisticated strategies for calculating, in order to get out of the Counting Trap.

Aspects of learning to count

These include:

- **recitation** – learning the number names and reciting them in sequence
- **one-to-one correspondence** – learning to synchronize each number with one object counted
- **cardinality** – understanding that the last number in a count represents the quantity in the group (e.g. 1, 2, 3, 4 so there are 4)
- **ordinality** – understanding that the last number in a count represents the place in a sequence (e.g. there are 4 so the last one is the fourth one).
- **place value** – understanding that the position of a digit in a number affects its value.

Place value and the principle of exchange

Many children find the concept of place value very difficult. Firstly they need to undertand the principle of exchange, that several items can be exchanged for, or represented by, one item of greater value. For example, 10 one pence coins equals one 10p coin; 7 days equals 1 week. Secondly they need to understand the structure of the 10 based sytem and the repeated pattern of hundreds, tens and units (HTU) within larger numbers.

Relating the counting words to the numbers is complicated by the fact that two symbols, for example 1 and 0 in the number 10, are represented by the single word 'ten'.

Numbers are read from left to right but English children have a particular difficulty because the words for 'teen' numbers appear to be read from right to left, for example 14 is **four**teen.

What causes problems in learning to count?

Difficulties occur when young children persist in learning to count as a string of sounds without being aware of the individual words as separate entities.

Children who are dyslexic and dyspraxic may have memory vulnerabilities and find learning to count a huge burden on their memory system. The development of counting overall can be delayed as well as their counting efficiency being compromised. The whole process may be weakly automatized. This means that they may not be able to continue counting on from any number, and they may have to start the count from the beginning each time. Sometimes they do not know which number to start counting on from – e.g. Asked to count on from 13, they are unsure whether to start the count at 13 or 14.

They may have **enumeration** difficulties with problems learning to synchronize number names with objects. Dyspraxic children may count scattered objects in a disorganized way without employing an efficient strategy such as moving each item to one side as it is counted. Most young children use their fingers. Dyspraxic children may be clumsy when using this strategy, leading to persistent miscounting.

Persistent miscounting may mean that they fail to grasp the stability of the quantity in a collection. This may lead to difficulty acquiring a sense of number. It then becomes hard to pay attention to patterns within and connections between numbers because the information appears inconsistent as it changes each time it is counted.

> **Summary of what can go wrong**
> - There may be a failure to grasp one-to-one correspondence.
> - There may be a unitary concept of number so they are trapped at a level of counting in ones and do not see number relationships.
> - They may remain in 'the Counting Trap'.
> - They may be unable to remember number facts.
> - They do not know which number to start counting from.
> - Lack of understanding of the principle of exchange and the place value system.

Dyscalculia and co-occurring conditions

This book provides an outline of the ways in which dyscalculia and co-occurring conditions affect maths learning. Educators need to be aware of the 'cocktail' of difficulties that may lie beneath mathematical difficulties. These include:

- specific language delay
- dyscalculia
- dyslexia
- dyspraxia
- maths anxiety
- attention deficit disorder (ADD) or with hyperactivity (ADHD)
- understanding and using the language of maths.

Specific language delay

Many children have language delays which will affect their ability to learn new vocabulary and acquire new concepts. Some of the vocabulary and concepts will be related to maths. Their difficulties may be with understanding language, or expressing themselves using language.

Children with language delays are likely to be slower to develop mathematical knowledge and skills than those without the same difficulties.

If a child has difficulty with the language of maths, it must then be considered whether they have a general language difficulty or a specific difficulty with the language of maths and maths-related words. This may need to be investigated by a speech and language therapist.

Dyscalculics, by contrast, are more likely to show normal language abilities apart from language related to mathematical concepts. This often includes any language that mentions words related to numbers. This area requires further research.

Dyscalculia

Dyscalculia affects the ability to acquire numeracy. Other terms may be used such as mathematical disability, arithmetic learning disability, and number fact disorder.

The field of dyscalculia is still in its infancy, compared with the state of the current acceptance and understanding of dyslexia. A qualitative assessment is going to be useful if it aims to analyse various critical areas and skills in mathematics and then suggests how the child's knowledge and skills can be developed, based on the evidence found.

Dyslexia

"Dyslexia is a learning difficulty that primarily affects the skills involved in accurate and fluent word reading and spelling.

Characteristic features of dyslexia are difficulties in phonological awareness, verbal memory and verbal processing speed.

Dyslexia occurs across the range of intellectual abilities.

It is best thought of as a continuum, not a distinct category, and there are no clear cut-off points.

Co-occurring difficulties may be seen in aspects of language, motor co-ordination, mental calculation, concentration and personal organisation, but these are not, by themselves, markers of dyslexia.

A good indication of the severity and persistence of dyslexic difficulties can be gained by examining how the individual responds or has responded to well-founded intervention" (Rose 2009).

What aspects of maths are affected by being dyslexic?

Language Dyslexics with auditory memory weaknesses often learn to speak later than other children. New vocabulary is acquired more slowly, so the language of maths is also affected. For example, words such as add, plus and total will take these children longer than the non-dyslexics to acquire. Once new information is learnt these children may use it as effectively as many of their peers, depending on their levels of verbal intelligence.

Left–right orientation Dyslexics often have a poor sense of left and right and up and down as well as a problem with using these directional words. Column work in maths requires good spatial orientation skills because children have to work from the right-hand units column to the left tens column, for example. They may get confused because mental maths in number sentences involves recording from left to right.

Sequencing difficulties Many dyslexics have difficulties learning sequential information and perceiving patterns of sequences. Sequential information includes such items as the days of the week, and the months of the year as well as learning the counting sequence and following mathematical procedures.

Memory weaknesses Many dyslexics have either auditory memory weaknesses or visual memory weaknesses. Sometimes both memory channels may be affected.

Auditory memory weaknesses will affect remembering mental maths questions. Visual memory weaknesses could limit the child's ability to develop visual images in their mind for use as a virtual thinking tool, when the concrete materials are not present. These children may have working memory constraints which will affect their ability to solve multi-stage calculations by limiting the amount of information that can be borne in mind while working on the problem. They will take longer to acquire new information. Their memory limitations will affect the long-term retention of the learnt material which may 'drop out' of their memory quite easily if not regularly revised.

Processing speed They may be slow to take in orally and visually presented information so the speed of presentation of the teacher may be too fast for them.

Visual and spatial awareness This may affect their ability to select what is important from a body of text so skimming and scanning text or numbers may be hard. They may also get lost finding their place on a page and returning to it.

Weak conceptual ability They may not easily grasp or retain new number concepts. Teaching sessions may not contain sufficient revision for a vulnerable individual.

Reading and writing Many dyslexics may be relatively good at maths but underachieve because they cannot read the questions. Poor spelling may inhibit their ability to write some answers down.

Dyspraxia

'Developmental dyspraxia, also known as Developmental Co-ordination Disorder (DCD), is characterized by the inability to carry out and plan sequences of coordinated movements to achieve an objective' (Kirby 2009).

What aspects of maths are affected by being dyspraxic?

Gross motor skills Gross motor skills are those that control large muscle movements and weaknesses may make planning and combining actions difficult, such as copying from the board. The acts of co-ordinating the movements and locating the right position on the page may make the process slow and laborious. The result may contain omissions and inaccuracies.

Eye-muscle tracking could also cause difficulties with copying from the board and difficulties reading a text fluently. This should be checked by a qualified optometrist rather than an optician.

Fine motor skills Poor fine motor skills may affect small muscle movements for writing numbers and words. This may result in poorly presented and untidy work. The poor layout of work may lead to unforced errors being made.

Speech difficulties: problems with articulating words Children who have speech difficulties may find it hard to pronounce multisyllabic and new words clearly. Poor auditory discrimination may affect crucial maths words such as the differentiation between thirteen and thirty. They may have trouble understanding similar words such as friction and fraction as well as using them to express their ideas.

Body image and body awareness Children with a poor sense of their own body may find it difficult to use their fingers for counting and may positively avoid doing so. They may not be aware of how many fingers they have, in spite of counting them frequently, and of where their fingers are in space. This is often referred to as finger agnosia. This may force them to try to do all their maths 'in their heads', without success.

Organizational skills Those affected may have difficulties getting started with their work because they are unable to organize their thoughts or to make plans on where to start. They find it hard to work in the structured way that maths in particular demands.

Visual perception Dyspraxic children may have difficulty making sense of visually presented material and even more problems copying this kind of material from the board. They may often lose their place and make frequent omissions when copying, in spite of having good visual acuity.

Concentration Dyspraxic children may find it hard to sit still because doing so requires conscious effort on their part. This makes attending to the lesson and staying on task difficult. They may suffer from mental and physical fatigue sooner than others because of the extra effort required to work and they may need to wriggle and fiddle.

Sensory integration Some children may have difficulties processing the feedback from their different senses and this may lead to distractions and difficulties focusing entirely on the task in hand.

Maths anxiety

Maths anxiety may affect maths performance or be caused by fear of maths through the difficulties themselves. The levels may rise to the point where it affects the child's ability to show what they can do in maths. It can actually rise to a point or a level where it paralyses their ability to perform even simple maths operations. Some children may refuse to do any maths at all or to be assessed. Many children experiencing significant maths difficulties are anxious. Teaching needs to take this into account and make sure that learning maths is an enjoyable and positive experience.

Some children may need help from a school counsellor or the child's family doctor before teaching can start. Others may benefit from experiencing some small successes in maths which in turn increases their self-belief about their ability to succeed in maths.

Attention deficit disorder (ADD)

ADD can be seen as a state of mind where tangential thoughts or actions occur that are not relevant to the immediate situation. Children with ADD rarely experience pauses in their thoughts, actions or responses to questions and tend to be impulsive.

If a degree of hyperactivity is also involved, the condition can be described as attention deficit hyperactivity disorder (ADHD) and extraneous movements will be observed. This might be swinging legs, fiddling with any object within reach, or leaving the seat to explore something that has caught their attention. An assessor may find himself or herself subconsciously or consciously responding to the child in order not to lose their attention, and may not be able to attend fully to recording their own observations.

If a child is known to have ADD or ADHD it is advisable to make an audio recording of the session in order to minimize the risk of losing the child's co-operation. By recording the session, the assessor can focus on the child rather than on writing down what is observed.

Understanding and using the language of maths

For some children maths can seem like a foreign language. Words used in everyday language have different meanings when applied to numeracy. (For example, 'difference' in everyday life indicates ways in which things are not the same as each other, whereas in maths it may mean subtraction.) Children can be very confused by even basic concepts such as 'more than' and 'less than', especially if they have problems with sequencing or left and right confusion.

Young children acquiring oral language gradually come to understand that words have multiple meanings, and acquiring appropriate maths language needs to be an interactive conversation between teachers and children. The assessment seeks to find out if the child is able to understand the different meanings of words when they relate to mathematics.

3

An overview of The Dyscalculia Assessment

The assessment is conducted in an informal way. It is important to be sensitive to the child's self-esteem at all times during the investigation.

Information is collected from three areas:
- an introductory conversation with the child
- a detailed investigation of basic numeracy to find out what the child can do
- information from other sources – parents, teachers, educational psychologists and other professionals.

How are pupils selected for assessment?

The assessment is useful for children who are:
- experiencing difficulties in maths, especially those who seem to have a poor sense of number; this may include poor ability to estimate quantities or the range of possible answers
- persistently counting on their fingers in spite of encouragement and training in other strategies
- suspected to be dyscalculic or those with other specific learning difficulties.

The assessment will be most useful when there is a significant discrepancy between the child's general intellectual level and their attainment in maths. This can be identified by comparing maths ability with other skills such as verbal abilities and literacy attainments.

What evidence does The Dyscalculia Assessment give?

The assessment provides evidence about:
- the child's ability to work with numbers in a way that shows if there is a developing sense of quantity and estimation abilities
- their knowledge of maths facts and possible strategies appropriate to the task presented
- fundamental areas of maths that the child needs help with, such as counting, or place value
- the child's sense of number. This refers to the child's awareness or 'feel' for the quantities represented by the counting numbers 1 to 9, and how they compare with each other in terms of size. This is often referred to as 'number sense'.

The information gained will enable the teacher to devise a maths intervention plan linked to the developmental stage of the child's maths. The results are not standardized because they relate only to the child assessed. However, the results do enable comparisons with other children for the purposes of grouping children for teaching. A Summary Maths Profile sheet is included in Appendix 4.

What information is the assessor looking for?

The assessor is looking for:
- what the child knows
- what the child can do
- how the child reasons about the maths
- the child's ability to talk about what they are doing

- the child's level of calculation competence
- any strategies that the child uses.

In addition the assessor will note general things that give an indication of how the child feels about learning in general and more specifically about maths. Indicators of the child's state of mind include:
- level of confidence (gauged from manner of speech and eye contact)
- level of anxiety (shown by posture, body language and appearance).

Social, emotional and language factors

- Is the child anxious or uncooperative in the maths lesson? A child may have turned off maths through failure, through not understanding, through anxiety or depression about maths.
- Is the child bringing another language to the lesson? Are they translating from another language? If they learnt maths elsewhere their maths language and vocabulary may be in another language, even if their social English is competent.

Where should a teaching plan start?

Teaching should start at the most basic level where difficulties were found during the assessment. However, with some older children it may be advisable to work on something emotionally acceptable to them, such as tables, and build in more fundamental skills, such as bridging, to support the tables work.

Overview of The Dyscalculia Assessment

1. Introductory conversation with the child

The assessor talks to the child about what they like and do not like about school, what they enjoy, what they think and feel about maths, which aspects they think they can do, and which aspects they find difficult.

2. Assessment: a structured investigation

The assessment is not timed. It is designed to encourage the child to talk about what they are doing and how they are thinking. It is **structured** with suggested wording to make it easy to use; however, the wording is not rigid and the assessor may use his or her judgement to make changes. It is essential that the meaning is clear to each child and all questions are kept short.

The child should be as relaxed as possible and enjoy the experience, with plenty of encouragement given during the meeting. The child is likely to have experienced repeated failure in maths and may have developed a negative attitude to the subject. It is essential to make the assessment as enjoyable as possible. Positive feedback can be given without telling the child whether they are right; indeed not indicating whether an answer or explanation is right or wrong is an important part of the delivery to maintain their self-esteem and co-operation.

Listening to and watching the child very carefully is an essential part of the investigation. Try to work out how the child interprets what you say because words often have specific meanings in maths which are different from everyday use. (For example, unit is a position in place value but may mean a kitchen cupboard in everyday situations.)

The assessment will take about one hour, less with a very young child of five or six years. However, you do not need to do it all in one session; it can be conducted over several sessions. If a pupil has good reasoning ability with basic number work this can be quickly established. Then the assessor can move on to parts that are more challenging such as calculation. However, experience has shown that for children with low numeracy the difficulties are likely to lie in their basic sense of number, such as estimating and sense of quantity. These areas are rarely fully explored. Some pupils may not need to do the whole assessment. Carefully note any basic counting difficulties and other fundamental errors. If the pupil makes two or three errors in a section, stop and move to the next section. The first section where errors are detected will probably form the starting point for intervention so it is not strictly necessary to complete the whole assessment.

3. Information from other sources

Information from parents, teachers and other professionals will help form a whole picture of the child's difficulties. The results of any standardized tests which have been done should be summarized to help give a more complete picture

Educational assessments

Educational or clinical psychologists[1] conduct assessments to explore a child's intellectual abilities and functioning. The most widely used is the WISC IV. There is a variety of diagnostic assessments available for use by teachers such as the Gillham and Hesse (2001) Basic Number Screening Test. These assessments may investigate some of the following areas:

- Verbal intelligence looks at general knowledge, thinking skills, vocabulary, common sense and word definitions.
- Non-verbal intelligence assesses copying two-dimensional designs, categorizing pictures, completing visual patterns and completing drawings of common objects which have missing parts.
- Memory tests involving auditory and visual memory skills.
- Attainments in literacy and numeracy.
- The child's verbal and non verbal levels can be compared with their levels achieved in literacy and numeracy. The assessment may indicate a discrepancy between the child's intelligence and their attainments at school. It also may indentify positive signs of specific learning difficulties.
- Other factors may be noted: ADD/ADHD, maths anxiety.

Physiotherapy assessments

These investigate the child's development of gross motor skills. These are the skills involved in large muscle movements such as kicking a ball.

Occupational therapy assessments

These explore the development of the child's fine motor skills. These are the skills involved in small muscle movements such as handwriting.

Speech and language assessments

These investigate speech (i.e. the way the child pronounces words), and the way the child uses language (i.e. how the child understands words and expresses themselves).

Assessment: Key points
- The assessment is a friendly, informal assessment.
- It collects information from three areas:
  - information from other sources – parents, teachers, educational psychologists
  - introductory conversation with the child – what they like and dislike about maths
  - The Dyscalculia Assessment – a structured investigation.
- It leads to understanding how a child reasons about numbers and what they know in key areas of numeracy.
- It provides information to develop a teaching plan.
- Observe carefully and record what the child does and what they say.
- Stop after two or three errors in each section to avoid provoking anxiety.

Note

1. Educational psychologists work in an educational setting. Clinical psychologists work in a clinical setting but may be looking at educational factors.

Top Tips **for a successful assessment**

- Look at the whole child rather than just their mathematical ability.
- Remember to smile and be encouraging throughout the investigation.
- If a child does not know you, greet them with a friendly smile and tell them your first name. Give them permission to call you by your first name. Tell them to take a seat for a few minutes and if they are with a parent they can look at an enjoyable book. Photographs of animals are always popular.
- Conduct the assessment in a room that is tidy, reasonably empty and devoid of distractions.
- Make sure that your table is completely clear to avoid distracting the child. Some children will grab anything on a table. Put any equipment you need on a separate table to the side.
- Make sure that the chair and table are the right height for the child so that their feet are firmly on the floor or on a footstool.
- Have a supply of stickers to give to the child to encourage them.
- You do not have to do the whole assessment: stop after two or three errors in each section and move to the next section if appropriate.
- Start the session with an ice-breaking activity by allowing the child to play with a timer, or use an unusual or interesting pencil sharpener. What is suitable will depend on the age of the child. This should not last more than a few minutes.
- Have a short relaxed chat with them. Discuss general topics such as pets, sports teams and brothers and sisters. Tell them that they have come to see you about their maths but this is not a test. Explain to them that you want to find out what they can do and if something is difficult then you will move on to something different.
- Avoid getting involved in tangential questions such as the child asking: 'Where do you live?'
- Notice their demeanour. Some children have difficulty making eye contact; others may rock on the chair. Encourage them to sit calmly on the chair.
- Look for signs of anxiety such as their appearance: chewed cuffs, bitten nails, fiddling with clothing. These children will need extra reassurance. Sometimes they will ask for reassurance that what they have done is good or correct. Give them praise and encouragement, but avoid telling them if something is right or wrong.
- Notice their level of concentration. Some children may be impulsive and rush their answers. Others may start to wriggle and get up and move to touch other things in the room. This means that the assessment will have to be conducted over several short sessions. It may indicate a primary concentration difficulty – the foundation of some of their difficulties may stem from their impulsivity or distractibility.
- Do not point out or refer to any mistakes. If a child makes repeated errors move on to the next section. When they struggle it is permissible to say: 'That seems a bit hard. Let's do something else.'
- If children ask for counters and other concrete materials that have not been provided, encourage them to do their best without extra materials. Ask them what equipment they like to use at school if this comes up.
- In most of the assessment the child is not asked to write anything but they may choose to do so. If they choose to write something down it may suggest that they find it hard to keep information in their mind, perhaps because they have a weak auditory memory or they may have been trained to record their thinking. Note the method of recording or calculating the child chooses to use, such as tally marks, number lines or column arithmetic.

4

The Dyscalculia Assessment

This chapter covers the following:

Equipment for the assessment

Equipment: Counters (glass nuggets recommended), pencil, paper, dice, squared paper (1 cm²), The Dyscalculia Assessment recording sheet, small circular stickers, reward stickers.

Extra forms available at: http://education.emersonbabtie.continuumbooks.com

General instructions

The assessment consists of two parts:

- A Background Questionnaire which forms the basis of an **initial discussion** with the child about their attitude to school and mathematics.
- The Dyscalculia Assessment is a **detailed investigation** of basic numeracy. A suggested script is provided along with space to record the findings.

The aim of the assessment is to find out what the child **can** do and **how** they reach their answers.

It is important that the child is relaxed and given enough time to talk. A key goal of the investigation is to find out whether they are able to explain how they are thinking. This is not a test; it is an investigation to find out what the child can do.

The instructions on the left-hand pages contain a suggested script, in italics, for the assessor. This is given as a guide. It is not essential to keep to the exact words, but it is essential to make your meaning clear. It is important that questions and instructions are clear and not too long. You may wish to change the wording, but make sure that you use language that is simple without being patronizing. Some children have poor memories so cannot easily process long sentences and complex language.

It is important to note down answers and observations during the discussion. (A sample template has been provided.) Notes need to be made discreetly because pupils will want to know what you are writing about them. In some cases it might be helpful to use a tape recorder. The report should be written up as soon as possible after the assessment while the session is still clear in your mind.

Chapter 5 discusses how to interpret problems that emerge from the assessment and how to overcome them.

Conducting the assessment

- Start with an empty table.
- Get the child to relax.
- Suggested script for the assessor is in italics.
- Encourage the child to talk about what they are doing and thinking.
- Give the child enough time to answer.
- Stop after two or three errors in each section and then move to the next section.
- Observe levels of anxiety throughout. Take a break or stop if the child is very anxious.
- If the child really struggles with early sections, do not proceed to the end of the investigation.
- Give non-specific praise in the form of encouraging comments. Do not give feedback about right or wrong responses.
- Record information and write up as soon as possible after the assessment.

What you are looking for in the assessment

You need to find out what the child knows, what they can do, and how they think about it. This involves giving the child things to do and asking them to tell you what they know and what strategies they are using. A useful aim is to determine whether they tend to try to remember answers off by heart, or whether they tend to work most things out. Many children will of course use a mixture of both.

Knowledge is what they know. For example, they may know 'off by heart' how to count accurately, essential number bonds and multiplication facts. They should also understand the place-value system and the principle of exchange.

Strategies are ways of achieving an answer by using knowledge and applying it in other situations. Strategies used in calculation include using fingers, tally marks, step-counting, bridging through ten and number lines. Not all strategies are efficient. Using fingers to count in ones is a strategy that quickly becomes very inefficient as the numbers get bigger. On the other hand, using knowledge of the 10 times and 5 times tables to derive all the other multiplication facts by reasoning is a very valuable strategy.

Strategies are useful if children understand them and can apply them. If a child has been taught a strategy and it works for them, allow them to use it but watch out for rote-learnt strategies which may be applied incorrectly because children have not remembered them accurately. If a child has used a strategy, remember to ask what the answer is at the end of the count or calculation. You may find that they have to start all over again because they do not understand what they are doing.

Finger counting

Children need to use their fingers to count initially. According to Stanislas Dehaene (1997) 'finger counting is an important precursor to learning base 10'. However, children need to develop more efficient strategies such as chunking or following patterns.

Observe carefully how children use their fingers. Using them to keep track of the number of groups being added in multiplication is an efficient use of fingers. However, children who have become caught in the Counting Trap (see page 6) use their fingers to count large quantities of ones. This is inefficient and often inaccurate as children become muddled about which fingers they have counted when dealing with large numbers.

Some children cannot use their fingers effectively. This might be due to motor coordination difficulties, sometimes known as developmental coordination disorder or dyspraxia. Some research has shown that some children may suffer from finger agnosia. This means that they are unaware of the number of fingers that they have and find it difficult to be sure of where their fingers are in space (Dehaene 1997).

Finger counting: some questions to consider
- Do they persistently miscount their fingers?
- Do they know they have five fingers on one hand and five on the other?
- Do they move their fingers but count inaccurately, showing a lack of one-to-one correspondence?
- Do they need to touch each finger as they count?
- Do they use the other hand to touch each finger or do they use other body parts such as nose or chin?

Subvocalizing

This means talking under your breath. You may see the child's lips moving slightly but they may try to cover up any outward sign. Often they will combine subvocalizing to count in ones with minimal finger movement. You can only be certain if they are subvocalizing if you ask them. Explain that you are interested in finding out how they think about maths. Make sure you reassure them that it is perfectly alright to count under their breath, or to use their fingers.

Subvocalizing is not wrong. Talking through what they are doing is exactly what you want the child to do; however, they should be reasoning to help develop their thinking, not simply rote counting.

Mantras

Some children have learnt mantras to help them remember facts or to calculate mentally. These may be helpful if they are remembered correctly. However, some can be quite complicated and lead to problems if they forget parts or misapply them.

Example of a mantra for mental calculation: 'Five in my head [points to head and touches it] and three fingers up [puts hand with three fingers up]'. Says again: 'Five in my head [touches head] six, seven, eight [touches each finger as counts six, seven, eight]'.

Tally marks

||||||| ⊦⊦⊦⊦ ||

Some children need to write calculations in tally marks before they can attempt them. If they group tallies into fives, this is evidence of understanding of a structure. However, many children will use individual tallies with no apparent structure. This may be evidence that they are caught in the Counting Trap or unsure of the counting sequence.

Visualizing

Visualizing means imagining an image in your head. If a child is silent and appears to be staring into space or looking up at the ceiling, they are probably imaging pictures which may be a line of numerals or a moving image rather like a video. One way to find out is to ask them if they are 'seeing something in their head' and if they can describe it to you.

Counting all

Starting counting in ones from the first number in a calculation is evidence of very poor number sense.

Counting on

This involves starting with a number and counting on from that number in ones. Children need this ability, but they should develop more efficient calculating strategies. A small development would be to start counting from the larger number.

Key number bonds

Number bonds are two numbers that, added together, make another number. The number bonds of the doubles, near doubles, bonds of ten and multiplication by 10 are the basis of efficient calculation strategies.

Step-counting

This is counting forwards or backwards in groups. Children should be able to step-count in tens, fives and twos. It is useful but not essential to be able to step-count in threes and fours. Step-counting numbers greater than five will probably be too difficult for children with a memory weakness.

Bridging

Bridging through ten, or a multiple of ten, is a very useful calculation strategy. Ten is used as a 'stepping stone' to add two single-digit numbers where the answer will be more than ten. Example: $5 + 8 = (5 + 5) + 3 = 10 + 3 = 13$. Children need to know the bonds of ten to use this strategy effectively.

Reasoning from known facts

Reasoning from known facts to derive other facts can be an effective way of calculating for children with poor memories. It is only possible to use this strategy if you understand the place-value system and the principle of exchange. It helps children develop a 'feel' for numbers.

Key facts

The key facts are: bonds of ten, doubles facts, and 10× every table.

The other facts can be derived from these key facts. For example if 10 eights are eighty then 5 eights can be derived by finding half of 80. Of course it is better to be able to recall more facts, but it is not essential provided that you understand how numbers can be combined and partitioned and how the place-value system works. It is essential that they explain their reasoning whenever they derive new facts. By doing so they will become more efficient at using reasoning strategies and find that they start to remember more facts. It takes a very long time but is well worth the effort.

Recording evidence

Make discreet notes on the assessment form provided. The topic is described briefly at the top of the page. The Questions column on the left is a list of the tasks required. The Star/tick column is to check off each item as it is completed. This will enable you to quickly review the child's knowledge of a topic. Use a star instead of a cross to draw attention to an error or problem. This will enable you to review the child's knowledge of a topic. The Comments and observations space is for writing brief notes that will provide the evidence from which to formulate a teaching plan. The tick checklist at the bottom of each page provides a quick summary of strategies the child may use. This will help highlight areas to target in the personalized plan for the child.

<table>
<tr>
<td colspan="3">Topic
Brief description of topic being assessed.</td>
</tr>
<tr>
<td>Questions
Summary of questions to be asked.</td>
<td>Star/tick
*   error
✓   item
     completed</td>
<td>Comments and observations
Brief notes about the child's responses. Include notes about attitude and fluency as well as the mathematical knowledge and strategies.</td>
</tr>
</table>

Fingers	☐	Subvocalizing	☐	Counting all	☐
Counting on	☐	Step-counting	☐	Looking into space	☐
Reasoning from known facts	☐	Can't explain	☐		

Summary Maths Profile

When the assessment is completed, fill in the Summary Maths Profile provided in Appendix 4 (page 165) for a quick reminder of what the child knows and which areas need attention.

**The Dyscalculia Assessment
Summary Maths Profile**

Name ....
Date of Assessment..
Date of Birth ....
Age at Assessment ....

NUMBER SENSE AND COUNTING		CALCULATION		PLACE VALUE	
Subitizing	☐☐☐☐☐☐	**Add** one more +1 two more +2	☐☐☐	**Principle of exchange**	☐☐

Estimation:
    up to10
    more than 10
			☐☐	**10 plus a single digit/Tens plus**
				10 plus a single digit (10 + n)
				tens plus a single digit (20 + n)
				Bridging:
				units + units (e.g. 8 + 5)
					☐
					☐
					☐☐
					☐

Counting: forwards in 1s	☐☐	**Subtract** one less − 1 two less − 2	☐☐		

Group matching

The Group Grid makes it easy to group children at similar educational needs/learning stages using colour coding. The information from the Summary Maths Profile is entered on a spreadsheet using a traffic-light system – green if the child's knowledge is secure, amber if they are unsure, red if their knowledge is weak. (See example in Appendix 4, page 166.)

Background Questionnaire

An initial discussion

It is important to talk to the child before the assessment to try to ensure that they are relaxed before they start. Maths anxiety is well known to reduce most children's ability to show what they can do in maths and may result in unforced errors occurring.

Fill in the personal details with information from the parents. Ask the child how old they are and when their birthday is. It is useful to know whether the child knows this information because it relates to their knowledge of maths in the real world.

General observations

1. Anxiety levels

Look for signs of general anxiety in the child's attitude and physical appearance:

- chewed cuffs
- bitten nails
- fiddling with clothing
- poor eye contact
- wriggling in their seat
- wringing hands
- speaking very softly and timidly.

Constantly asking for or looking for reassurance is also a sign of anxiety. These children will need extra reassurance and sometimes they will ask for it in order to be sure that what they have done is good or correct. Give them praise and encouragement.

2. Attention levels

The child may be unable to sit still or remain seated on the chair. If they get up and move around the room and touch things, this is an indication of poor concentration, an inability to follow instructions, lack of obedience, deliberate defiance or oppositional behaviour. It could also be indicative of sensory-motor difficulties which would mean that they need to move around to increase the information they are receiving about where their bodies are in space.

During the assessment the child may be impulsive and rush the answers. This may be caused by anxiety and wanting to complete the task as quickly as possible. However, it may be an indication of an attention deficit disorder.

Are they able to focus on the task in hand? A child who covers one eye with hair or a hand may be inattentive or it may be a sign of a visual difficulty which would need professional investigation.

The child may be verbally impulsive. This means that they ask tangential questions unrelated to the task, or too many questions that are time wasting. They may also answer in a rambling fashion which may indicate expressive language weaknesses. These could be investigated further by a speech and language therapist.

Background Questionnaire

Name: _____

Date of birth: _____ Age at assessment: _____

Date of assessment: _____

Contact information

Name of parent or guardian: _____

Address: _____

Telephone: _____

Email: _____

General observations:

1. Anxiety levels (signs observed)

2. Attention levels (observations made)

Attitudes to school and maths

1. How is school work in general?

Do you like school? How do you get on with your school work? Which subject do you like best? Are there any subjects you don't like?

Find out about their attitude to school and maths by asking a series of open questions which do not suggest any particular answer.

2. How is maths in particular?

How do you get on with maths at school? Are there some parts of your maths lessons that you enjoy? How do you feel about maths now and how did you feel in the past? Are you the sort of person who knows a lot of maths off by heart or do you have to work most of it out?

If they say they don't know, assessor responds: *Don't worry. We will find out as we talk.*

3. What do you like doing and what don't you like doing in maths?

Some children enjoy counting because they have good memories but may dislike work with shapes because they may have a visual perceptual difficulty. Others may hate counting because they have a sequential memory weakness, but enjoy work with shapes because they have good visual abilities.

Attitudes to school and maths

1. How is school work in general?

2. How is maths in particular?

3. What do you like doing and what don't you like doing in maths?

The Dyscalculia Assessment

SECTION 1: NUMBER SENSE AND COUNTING

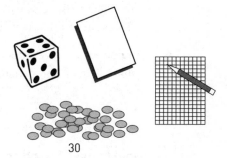

Equipment: 1 dice, at least 30 counters (same colour), pencil, squared paper (1 cm²), sheet of paper to cover counters.

Number sense

Very young children slowly develop number sense by repeatedly counting small groups of objects and establishing that the number of items in the group remains the same. In this way children develop a feel for the range of individual quantities, usually up to about ten items. This feel for quantities and the number words and written symbols which refer to them is usually described as basic number sense. This sense is relatively easily acquired by most children, especially for small quantities of three or four items. This instant recognition is known as the ability to subitize. Some children are not able to do this, and will count the items one by one (Yeo 2003).

Counting and the number system

This section of the assessment looks at children's ability to count forwards and backwards in ones, and to count in tens. This part checks if they have understanding of the tens-based nature of the number system. It also investigates if children have an awareness that the system can be built up of groups of 10 items, or 100 items, or 1000 items to infinity.

This assessment looks at the following areas:

- **Subitizing** is an innate skill that most young children have. Children should be able to recognize and say the correct number word for up to four objects without counting, when these objects are randomly scattered over a small area (such as half an A4 piece of paper).
- **Estimating** is the ability to guess roughly how many items there are in a group without counting. Children need to understand the concept of estimation as later they will need to estimate the approximate size of their answer before undertaking any formal calculations. This is a particularly important skill in the technological age where you need to be able to recognize whether a computer-generated result is sensible.
- **Oral counting** is the ability to say number words attached to a group of items as you count them one by one accurately.
- **Writing numbers** is the ability to record digits accurately to represent mapping the spoken word onto the written symbol for the number. This will indicate their understanding of place-value knowledge.
- **Reading numbers** is the ability to say the correct number words when presented with the written digits

> ### Remember
> - Make sure the atmosphere is friendly.
> - Note what the child knows, and what strategies they use for any counting.
> - Keep your language simple, with short sentences.
> - Stop after two or three errors and move on to the next section.

Number sense

- This section investigates the child's sense of number.
- It checks whether they have a feel for the size of a quantity of objects without counting them one by one. It explores early knowledge of the way the number system is structured in groups of tens.
- Does the child have a counting strategy?

Equipment: 1 dice, 30 counters (same colour), 1 cm² squared paper and pencil, blank sheet of paper.

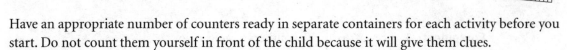

Have an appropriate number of counters ready in separate containers for each activity before you start. Do not count them yourself in front of the child because it will give them clues.

How to assess and record

- Note their answers on the assessment form on the facing page.
- Note any strategies they use.
- Make encouraging comments, but do not tell the child if they are right or wrong.

> - How do they check?
> - Do they use fingers?
> - Do they subvocalize?
> - Do they touch or move the counters as they count?
> - Are they using any strategy such as counting in twos?

Subitizing

Up to 4 counters

Show the child a single counter and let them look at it closely and feel it. Then put the counters out of sight.

I am going to put some counters on the table. You will only be able to look at them for a few seconds before telling me how many there are.

Put 2 counters out and then quickly cover them with a sheet of paper. *How many do you think there are?* Record response on the assessment form.

Scatter 4 counters. Cover them with paper after a few seconds. *How many do you think there are?*

> - Being able to identify quantities up to 4 is an important basic skill. Can they say how many there are without counting?

Estimating

5 to 10 counters

Estimating means making a sensible guess about how many things there are. Put out a small pile of counters – more than 5 but fewer than 10. Cover them quickly. *How many do you think there are?*

Now count how many there actually are.

10 to 20 counters

Repeat the exercise with between 10 and 20 counters. This time say: *Please move or touch the counters as you are counting them.*

More than 20 counters

Give the child more than 20 counters and say: *Count them into lines of tens; start the count again after each ten.*

How many are there? How do you know that?

> - Can they count in tens or do they need to count in ones?
> - Do they choose to leave a space between each ten counters?
> - Do they understand that numbers are arranged as a tens-based system and that numbers can be arranged in groups of ten with some left over?
> - Can they continue to count on from 10, or do they have to go back to the beginning and count all the counters?
>
> - Do they put out 9 instead of 10 counters before leaving a gap? Do not correct this. Observe whether they notice the error when they check it.
> - Example: 23 counters. Acceptable responses are: 'There are two lines of ten with three more'. 'There are 23'. 'There are two groups of ten with three left over'.

2

Number sense

- This section investigates the child's sense of number.
- It checks whether they have a feel for the size of a quantity of objects without counting them one by one. It explores early knowledge of the way the number system is structured in groups of tens.
- Does the child have a counting strategy?

Questions	Star/tick	Comments
Subitizing 2 4		
Estimating Less than 10 – estimate – count		
Between 10 and 20 – estimate – count		
More than 20 – estimate – move or touch as they count		
Put into lines of 10		

Fingers	☐	Subvocalizing	☐	Counting all	☐
Counting on	☐	Step-counting	☐	Looking into space	☐
Reasoning from known facts	☐	Can't explain	☐		

Counting and the number system

- Counting forms the basis of all calculation.
- Counting should be fluent without undue hesitation or pauses.
- The child should be able to count on from any number.

Oral counting

Before children can learn more efficient calculation strategies they need to be able to count effectively and accurately with flexibility and fluency.

Children should be able to say a sequence of numbers without pauses and without undue hesitation.

Counting forwards in ones

Count forwards until I ask you to stop. Stop them somewhere in the twenties, if they reach that far. After they have done some oral counting ask: *How do you know what number is next?*

Possible responses could be 'I use my fingers' or 'I see them in my head'. Some may say they just know off by heart.

- Note any errors, without the child being aware if possible.
- Does the child pause or seem to be thinking hard?
- Are they using a strategy such as counting on fingers or visualizing a number line?
- Eyes turned upwards are a possible sign of visualization.

Counting backwards in ones

Count from 10 back to zero.
Count from 15 back to zero.

If the previous sections were managed well ask for a count back from 20. *Count back from 20.*

Count back from 60. Only ask this if the child is confident counting back from 20. Stop the child at 46 if the count is accurate. If the count is not accurate stop the count when it becomes clear that they are muddled.

- Note the '-teen' pronunciation. If pronunciation is unclear, they may confuse the '-teen' and '-ty' numbers such as 14 and 40 because they cannot hear the difference between the endings.
- Poor auditory discrimination should alert the assessor to check that the hearing of the child has been tested at a health centre or clinic.

Counting and the number system

- Counting forms the basis of all calculation.
- Counting should be fluent without undue hesitation or pauses.
- The child should be able to count on from any number.

Questions	Star/tick	Comments
Counting forwards in ones		
In ones forward from 1		
In ones forward from arbitrary points 7, 16, 29		
Counting backwards in ones		
From 10 back to 0		
From 15 back to 0		
From 20 back to 0		

Fingers	☐	Subvocalizing	☐	Counting all	☐
Counting on	☐	Step-counting	☐	Looking into space	☐
Reasoning from known facts	☐	Can't explain	☐		

Counting – across the decades and step-counting

- The child should be able to count across the decade boundaries.
- They should be able to step-count in tens, twos and fives.
- They should be able to count forwards and short distances backwards.

Decade boundaries

Ask the child to count forwards from random points in the counting sequence. Choose examples that cross the decade boundaries. Example: The boundary between the twenties and thirties by counting from 26 to 32.

Now count forwards from 7. Stop them after 12. *Now count from 16.* Stop them when they reach 23. *Now count from 29.* Stop them at 34. *Now count from 76.* Stop them at 82. *Now count from 96.* Stop them after 104.

- Note any struggle. Do they seem to be thinking hard? Are they using a strategy such as visualizing?
- Do they count backwards more slowly?
- Note any hesitations or errors. Do they self-correct?

Counting forwards in tens

Now I want you to count forwards again. I want you to count in tens.

Counting backwards in tens

If the child is able to do this ask them to count backwards in tens.

- Note what happens at the decade boundary, especially for 90, 100, 110, etc. Do they switch back to counting in ones or counting in hundreds, sometimes known as an 'illegal count'?

Counting forwards in fives

Count forwards from 5 to 100 or beyond.

Now I want you to count in fives.

If the child is able to do this easily, stop them after 30 and ask them to start counting in fives from 80.

- Note any errors, but especially around 95, 100, 105.

Counting backwards in fives

If the child is able to do this ask them to count backwards in fives.

Counting in twos forwards to 30

Ask for a count in twos beyond 20. Ask how they are doing this. If this is easy, ask for a count in twos from 7 to see how flexible their counting skills are.

Counting backwards in twos

If the child is able to count forwards in twos ask them to count backwards in twos.

Counting – across the decades and step-counting

- The child should be able to count across the decade boundaries.
- They should be able to step-count in tens, twos and fives.
- They should be able to count forwards and short distances backwards.

Questions Decade boundaries	Star/tick	Comments
Counting forwards in tens In tens forwards to 100 or beyond If the above was easy, ask them to count in tens from a number such as 14.		
Counting backwards in 10s		
Counting forwards in fives In fives forwards from 5 to 100 or beyond		
Counting backwards in fives		
Counting in twos forwards to 30 In twos forwards to 30		
Counting backwards in twos		

Fingers	☐	Subvocalizing	☐	Counting all	☐
Counting on	☐	Step-counting	☐	Looking into space	☐
Reasoning from known facts	☐	Can't explain	☐		

End of the counting section. Pause for a brief chat and to choose another sticker, perhaps.

For extra forms go to: http://education.emersonbabtie.continuumbooks.com

Writing and reading numbers

- **Writing numbers:** writing numbers is harder than reading numbers and so precedes the reading numbers section. Remember to stop after two or three errors.
- **Reading numbers:** find the level of their automatic knowledge. Stop after responses cease to be automatic

Equipment: squared paper (1 cm²) and pencil.

Writing numbers

Give the pupil a piece of squared paper and pencil.

Write the numbers up to ten.

When they have done that say: *Can you write the numbers up to twenty?*

Write some more numbers. Give the following numbers one at a time. Do not rush. Stop after three errors.

27, 34, 68, 72, 90, 100, 101, 104, 110, 140, 238, 984, 1,000, 1,001, 1,947, 2,056, 3,709

Continue with higher numbers. Vary the zero position. If they are successful continue until a ceiling is found.

84,294   73,501   60,183   90,067   195,647
408,756   1,593,486   8,602,684

> - Are there any reversals when writing the -teens, as in 41 for 14? Do they write the -teen numbers by writing the 1 after they have written the unit digit? This shows that they have had previous difficulty with the order of writing the -teen numbers.

> - Do they write as they hear, showing lack of place-value structure knowledge, as in 100403 instead of 143?

> - Do they use any strategies, such as writing HTU (hundreds, tens, units) column headings for example?

Reading numbers

Find the level of their automatic knowledge. Stop after responses cease to be automatic.

Teacher writes one number and asks pupil to read it. Continue writing down numbers one by one. Increase the size as appropriate. Build up from single digits, asking them to read each number after you have written it.

4, 5, 7, 11, 13, 30, 17, 70, 84, 91, 100, 147, 207, 476, 670, 817

> - Note if they use any strategies (such as column headings).

If the child manages three-digit numbers, assess thousands, tens of thousands, and hundreds of thousands.

2,943   7,240   16,835   70,068   956,327

Writing and reading numbers

- **Writing numbers:** writing numbers is harder than reading numbers and so precedes the reading numbers section. Remember to stop after two or three errors.
- **Reading numbers:** find the level of their automatic knowledge. Stop after responses cease to be automatic.

Questions	Star/tick	Comments
Writing **Write numbers to 10** **Write numbers to 20** (Note any reversals such as 41 for 14) **Write numbers said by teacher** 27, 34, 68, 72, 90, 100, 101, 104, 110, 140, 238, 984, 1,000, 1,001, 1,947, 2,056, 3,709 If all correct continue with higher numbers. Vary zero position. 84,294, 73,501, 60,183, 90,067, 195,647, 408,756, 1,593,486, 8,602,684 *Reading* Teacher writes numbers one at a time. Child reads each one. Stop after responses cease to be automatic. 4, 5, 7, 11, 13, 30, 17, 70, 84, 91, 100, 147, 207, 476, 670, 817 If all correct then: 2,943, 7,240, 16,835, 70,068, 956,327		

Fingers	☐	Subvocalizing	☐	Counting all	☐
Counting on	☐	Step-counting	☐	Looking into space	☐
Reasoning from known facts	☐	Can't explain	☐		

End of writing and reading numbers section. Pause for brief chat. Choosing a sticker can be helpful.

For extra forms go to: http://education.emersonbabtie.continuumbooks.com

SECTION 2: CALCULATION

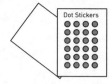

Equipment: 1 dice, squared paper (1 cm²) and pencil, small circular stickers and plain paper.

Early calculation

Early calculation is the ability to add one or two to a number, or subtract one or two from a number. Start with numbers below 10. If the pupil is successful with single-digit numbers, proceed to numbers between 10 and 20.

Doubles facts

Doubles facts are obtained by adding a number to itself. Children should know the doubles facts for each of the counting numbers to 10 + 10.

Examples of doubles facts are 2 + 2 = 4, 7 + 7 = 14.

Near doubles facts

Near doubling is adding adjacent numbers to each other.

Examples of near doubles facts are 3 + 4 = 7, 6 + 7 = 13.

Dot pattern-knowledge

Dot pattern-knowledge is the instant recognition of the conventional dice patterns (1–6) without counting.

Number bonds

Number bonds are the various ways a whole number can be split into parts.

Example: 5 is made of 1 + 4, 2 + 3, 3 + 2, 4 + 1 and 5 + 0.

The key number bonds are the doubles facts and near doubles facts and the bonds of ten.

The bonds of ten facts are crucial. They underpin calculation throughout the number system.

Automatic knowledge of the rest of the number bonds is helpful but some pupils may derive these from the key number bonds and doubles and near doubles facts or by bridging.

The calculation section investigates:

- doubles and near doubles facts
- number bonds from 1 to 9
- number bonds of 10
- number bonds through the decades
- number bonds of 100.

> **Remember:**
> - Make sure the atmosphere is friendly.
> - Note what the child knows.
> - Observe which strategies they use for calculation.
> - Keep your language simple and straightforward.
> - Stop after two or three errors.

Early calculation – addition: +1

- Investigate flexibility of counting on one more from any number.
- Start with numbers under 10. Only proceed to numbers between 10 and 20 if the pupil is successful with single-digit numbers.
- Use the terms 'more than', 'add', 'plus' to express addition in this part of the assessment.

Equipment: pencil, squared paper (1 cm²).

Addition: +1

Oral +1
Begin with oral questions.

What is 1 more than 5?
What is 4 add 1?
What is 7 plus 1?
What is 6 and 1?

> - Note what pupil does. Do they answer quickly without hesitation? Do they have to start counting all the numbers from the beginning of the sequence? Example: What is 4 add 1? Child responds 1, 2, 3, 4, 5.

If they succeed on two or three items proceed to the -teen numbers between 10 and 20.

What is 1 more than 11?
What is 12 plus 1?
What is 14 and 1?

> - Target '-teen' numbers with stem changing: <u>thir</u>teen and <u>fif</u>teen.

If they can do these check some higher numbers.

What is 1 more than 36?
What is 49 and 1?
What is 70 plus 1?

> - Do they get stuck at decade boundaries? Example: 39 + 1. The child responds 30 or 41.

Written +1
Assessor writes down the questions one at a time.
For each one says: *Can you do this for me? Write the answer.*

$4 + 1 =$
$6 + 1 =$

If appropriate proceed to higher numbers.
Write down the questions: *Can you do this for me? Write the answer.*

$28 + 1 =$ $\qquad$ $39 + 1 =$ $\qquad$ $80 + 1 =$

Early calculation – addition: +1

- Investigate flexibility of counting on one more from any number.
- Start with numbers under 10. Only proceed to numbers between 10 and 20 if the pupil is successful with single-digit numbers.
- Use the terms 'more than', 'add', 'plus' to express addition in this part of the assessment.

Questions	Star/tick	Comments
Addition 'More than, add, plus'		
Oral +1 *1 more than 5* *4 add 1* *7 plus 1* *6 and 1* *1 more than 11* *12 plus 1* *14 plus 1* *1 more than 36* *49 and 1* *70 plus 1*		
Written +1 4 + 1 = 6 + 1 = 28 + 1 39 + 1 80 + 1		

Fingers	☐	Subvocalizing	☐	Counting all	☐
Counting on	☐	Step-counting	☐	Looking into space	☐
Reasoning from known facts	☐	Can't explain	☐		

For extra forms go to: http://education.emersonbabtie.continuumbooks.com

Early calculation – addition: +2

- Investigate flexibility of counting on two.
- Start with numbers under 10. Only proceed to numbers between 10 and 20 if the pupil is successful with single-digit numbers.
- Use the terms 'more than', 'add', 'plus' to express addition in this part of the assessment.

Equipment: pencil, squared paper (1 cm²).

Addition: +2

Oral +2
Investigate counting on two more. The child says the answer.
What is 2 more than 6?
What is 5 plus 2?

If appropriate proceed to numbers between 10 and 20.
What is 2 more than 13?
What is 17 add 2?

If appropriate proceed to higher numbers.
What is 2 more than 39?
What is 67 add 2?

Written +2
Assessor writes down the questions one at a time and says:
Can you do this for me? Write the answer.
5 + 2 =
7 + 2 =

- Is the child unsure where to start counting on? Example: With 'one more' than 12 they are unsure whether the answer is 13 or 14.
- Do they have to start counting all the numbers from the beginning of the sequence? Example: What is 2 more than 5? The child responds 1, 2, 3, 4, 5, 6, 7.
- Do they understand what 'more than' means?
- Do they count on in ones?

If this is successful investigate numbers between 10 and 20.
11 + 2 =
13 + 2 =

If appropriate proceed to higher numbers with some crossing decade boundaries (e.g. 29, 30, 31).
43 + 2 =
29 + 2 =
59 + 2 =

Early calculation – addition: +2

- Investigate flexibility of counting on two.
- Start with numbers under 10. Only proceed to numbers between 10 and 20 if the pupil is successful with single-digit numbers.
- Use the terms 'more than', 'add', 'plus' to express addition in this part of the assessment.

Questions	Star/tick	Comments
Addition 'More than, add, plus'		
Oral +2 *2 more than 6* *5 plus 2* *2 more than 13* *17 add 2* *2 more than 39* *67 add 2*		
Written +2 5 + 2 = 7 + 2 = 11 + 2 = 13 + 2 = 43 + 2 = 29 + 2 = 59 + 2 =		

Fingers	☐	Subvocalizing	☐	Counting all	☐
Counting on	☐	Step-counting	☐	Looking into space	☐
Reasoning from known facts	☐	Can't explain	☐		

Early calculation – subtraction: –1, –2

- Investigate flexibility of counting back one or two from any number.
- Start with numbers under 10. Only proceed to numbers between 10 and 20 if the pupil is successful with single-digit numbers.
- Use the terms 'less than', 'take away', 'minus' to express subtraction in this part of the assessment.

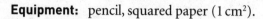

Equipment: pencil, squared paper (1 cm²).

Subtraction: –1, –2

Oral –1

Begin with oral questions.
What is 1 less than 3?
What is 7 take away 1?
What is 6 minus 1?

If they succeed on two or three items proceed to the -teen numbers between 10 and 20.
What is 1 less than 14?
What is 19 minus 1?
What is 16 take away 1?

Written –1

Assessor writes down the questions one at a time.
For each one say: *Can you do this for me? Write the answer.*
3 – 1 =
8 – 1 =
16 – 1 =
20 – 1 =

Oral –2

Assessor asks the child:
What is 2 less than 8?
What is 5 take away 2?
What is 17 minus 2?

- Does the child have difficulty counting backwards?
- Does the child find counting back two harder than counting back one?
- Does the child omit numbers?
- Does the child get stuck at crossover points? Example: Count 32, 31, 30, 39, 38.
- Do they count forwards to check number before counting backwards?
- Do they subvocalize?
- Do they use fingers?

Written –2

Write down the questions one at a
time. For each one say: *Can you do this one for me? Write the answer.*
9 – 2 =
15 – 2 =

Larger numbers: if the child is able to do all the above easily, ask a few questions using numbers in the higher decades.
47 – 2 =
51 – 2 =
70 – 2 =

Early calculation: subtraction –1, –2

- Investigate flexibility of counting back one or two from any number.
- Start with numbers under 10. Only proceed to numbers between 10 and 20 if the pupil is successful with single-digit numbers.
- Use the terms 'less than', 'take away', 'minus' to express subtraction in this part of the assessment.

Questions	Star/tick	Comments
Subtraction		
Oral –1		
1 less than 3		
7 take away 1		
6 minus 1		
1 less than 14		
19 minus 1		
16 take away 1		
Written –1		
3 – 1 =		
8 – 1 =		
16 – 1 =		
20 – 1 =		
Oral –2		
2 less than 8		
5 take away 2		
17 minus 2		
Written –2		
9 – 2 =		
15 – 2 =		
Higher numbers		
47 – 2 =		
51 – 2 =		
70 – 2 =		

Fingers	☐	Subvocalizing	☐	Counting all	☐
Counting on	☐	Step-counting	☐	Looking into space	☐
Reasoning from known facts	☐	Can't explain	☐		

For extra forms go to: http://education.emersonbabtie.continuumbooks.com

Doubles, e.g. 2 + 2

- A double is a number that is added to itself to obtain another number.
- Check rote knowledge or automatic recall of doubles facts.

Equipment: pencil, squared paper (1 cm²).

Written

We are going to look at the doubles numbers. I'm going to start with a nice one.

Assessor writes 2 + 2

What is 2 + 2?

If the child knows the answer, then say:

You know that one. Does that help you with 2 and 3?

> - If the child is able to explain that if 2 + 2 = 4 then 2 + 3 must be one more than 4 this indicates that they are thinking mathematically and reasoning about numbers at a basic level.

Assessor writes 2 + 3 =

If child says 'no' but gets 2 + 3 correct, ask them how they did it.

If child says yes, ask them how they did it.

A common response is 'It's just one more'.

Why is it just one more?

Let's do some more.

Write down the questions one at a time. Wait until the child has responded before writing the next one.

3 + 3 =

4 + 4 =

5 + 5 =

> - Are they deriving answers from known facts?
> - Do they count from one?
> - Are they calculating?
> - Do they use fingers?

Can you tell me another one like that?

Oral doubles

If the doubles to 5 + 5 are known, ask the higher doubles to 10 + 10 out of order.

What is 7 plus 7?

What is 9 plus 9?

What is 8 plus 8?

If the pupil does not know the answers, write them down.

If appropriate and the pupil is confident with lower numbers, ask:

What is 20 plus 20?

What is 30 plus 30?

What is 50 plus 50?

Doubles, e.g. 2 + 2

- A double is a number that is added to itself to obtain another number.
- Check rote knowledge or automatic recall of doubles facts.

Questions	Star/tick	Comments
Doubles		
2 + 2		
2 + 3		
3 + 3		
4 + 4		
5 + 5		
7 *plus* 7		
9 *plus* 9		
8 *plus* 8		
If appropriate		
20 *plus* 20		
30 *plus* 30		
50 *plus* 50		

Fingers	☐	Subvocalizing	☐	Counting all	☐
Counting on	☐	Step-counting	☐	Looking into space	☐
Reasoning from known facts	☐	Can't explain	☐		

For extra forms go to: http://education.emersonbabtie.continuumbooks.com

Near doubles, e.g. 3 + 4

- Near doubling is adding adjacent numbers to each other.
- Examples of near doubles facts are 3 + 4 = 7, 6 + 7 = 13.
- Check rote knowledge or automatic recall of doubles facts.

Equipment: pencil, squared paper (1 cm²).

Written

We are going to do some more questions.

Write down the questions one at a time. Wait until the child has responded before writing the next one.

Assessor writes down 2 + 3 =
> *What is 2 plus 3?*

Assessor writes down 3 + 4 =
> *What is 3 plus 4?*

Assessor writes down 4 + 5 =
> *What is 4 plus 5?*

If the responses are correct, ask: *How did you do that?*

If appropriate, continue with more difficult questions. You may write them down or ask the child orally.
> *What is 6 plus 7?*
> *What is 8 plus 9?*

- Observe how the child calculates each answer.
- Are they deriving answers from known facts, counting or calculating?
- Do they use a strategy that reflects that these are almost the same as doubles?
- Did they count on from the first number given?
- Did they find the largest number and count on?
- Did they use a doubles fact and count on one more? Did they use bridging for 6 + 7 (making the problem into (6 + 4) + 3)?
- Note any other strategy that has been taught or invented.

Near doubles, e.g. 3 + 4

- Near doubling is adding adjacent numbers to each other.
- Examples of near doubles facts are 3 + 4 = 7, 6 + 7 = 13.
- Check rote knowledge or automatic recall of doubles facts.

Questions	Star/tick	Comments
Near doubles, e.g. 3 + 4		
2 + 3		
3 + 4		
4 + 5		
If appropriate,		
6 + 7		
8 + 9		

Fingers	☐	Subvocalizing	☐	Counting all	☐
Counting on	☐	Step-counting	☐	Looking into space	☐
Reasoning from known facts	☐	Can't explain	☐		

For extra forms go to: http://education.emersonbabtie.continuumbooks.com

Dot pattern-knowledge

- Check if the child can recognize and draw the dot patterns 1–6 as found on a conventional dice. (Note if they can recognize the patterns without counting.)
- Encourage the child to use their knowledge of the dot patterns 1–6 to create new patterns of their own for the numbers 7, 8, 9 and 10.

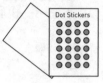

Equipment: 1 dice, squared paper (1 cm²) and pencil, small circular stickers and plain paper.

Dot patterns

Show the child a dice with the dot patterns 1–6.
   Have you played games with a dice like this?

- Do they have to count the dots?

Show the child the pattern of 3 on the dice. *What number is this?*
   Show the 5. *What number is this?*
   Show the 6. *What number is this?*
   I want you to draw some patterns.

Using squared paper, draw two dots to demonstrate what is required.
   This is the dot pattern of 2:

- If the child draws a pattern that is not a conventional dice pattern, make a note.
- Is the child able to draw the dots in a recognizable form? If not, further investigation of their visual and spatial skills by an occupational therapist may be necessary.

Show the child the dot pattern of 4 for a few seconds.
   Can you draw this?

Show the child the dot pattern of 6 for a few seconds.
   Can you draw this?

If the child drew 4 and 6 correctly, point out the doubles pattern.
   Can you see that 4 is made of 2 and 2?
   Can you see that 6 is made of 3 and 3?
   If you were going to make up a pattern of 8, how would you draw it?

- Accept any creative suggestion that combines two of the other dice patterns or a reasonable alternative. If they draw single lines of dots with no discernible pattern, this may indicate visual perceptual difficulties or poor pattern awareness.

Child draws pattern.
   What about a pattern of 10? Can you draw it?

Dot pattern-knowledge

- Check if the child can recognize and draw the dot patterns (1–6) as found on a conventional dice. (Note if they can recognize the patterns without counting.)
- Encourage the child to use their knowledge of dot patterns (1–6) to create new patterns of their own for the numbers 7, 8, 9 and 10.

Questions	Star/tick	Comments
Dot Patterns Teacher draws 2 dots to show the dot pattern.		
Child draws pattern for 4.		
Child draws pattern for 6.		
Look at the doubles patterns in 4 and 6.		
Child draws new doubles patterns.		
Doubles pattern for 8		
Doubles pattern for 10		

Fingers	☐	Subvocalizing	☐	Counting all	☐
Counting on	☐	Step-counting	☐	Looking into space	☐
Reasoning from known facts	☐	Can't explain	☐		

Number bonds 1 to 9

- Number bonds are two numbers that are combined to make another number: $2 + 3 = 5$.
- Investigate the child's knowledge of the structure of the numbers from 1 to 9.
- Key number bonds are doubles and near doubles.
- Other number bonds are the rest of the bonds for the numbers 1 to 9.

Equipment: squared paper (1 cm²) and pencil.

Key number bonds

Doubles and near doubles facts Example: Key facts for 6 are $3 + 3$ and key facts for 7 are $3 + 4$ or $4 + 3$.

Write these problems one at a time on the squared paper. Stop after two or three errors.

If the pupil cannot do the addition, try one subtraction before stopping.

Give an easy example:
$2 + \square = 3$

Addition (missing addends)

$2 + \square = 5$ $4 + \square = 8$

$3 + \square = 7$ $3 + \square = 6$

$4 + \square = 9$

- Do they use their fingers?
- Do they count on or back?
- Do they use knowledge of the number bonds? For example, if 7 is made from $4 + 3$ then $4 + 3 = 7$ and $7 - 4 = 3$.

Subtraction

$4 - 2 = \square$ $6 - 3 = \square$

$7 - 3 = \square$ $9 - 5 = \square$

Other number bonds

These comprise examples of the number bonds for the numbers 1 to 9 other than those made from doubles, e.g. $4 + 4$ and near doubles such as $4 + 3$.

Write these problems one at a time on the squared paper. Stop after two or three errors.

If the pupil cannot do the addition, try one subtraction before stopping.

- Do they count on?
- Do they count back? Are they using number-bonds knowledge? Example: $8 = 3 + 5$ and $5 + 3$.
- Are they using their fingers?

Addition (missing addends)

$4 + \square = 6$ $2 + \square = 9$

$1 + \square = 5$ $3 + \square = 8$

Subtraction

$9 - 7 = \square$ $5 - 4 = \square$

$8 - 2 = \square$ $7 - 5 = \square$

Number bonds 1 to 9

- Number bonds are two numbers that are combined to make another number: 2 + 3 = 5.
- Investigate the child's knowledge of the structure of the numbers from 1 to 9.
- Key number bonds are doubles and near doubles.
- Other number bonds are the rest of the bonds for the numbers 1 to 9.

Questions	Star/tick	Comments
Key number bonds *Written* *Addition (missing addends)* 2 + ☐ = 3 2 + ☐ = 5 4 + ☐ = 8 3 + ☐ = 7 3 + ☐ = 6 4 + ☐ = 9 *Subtraction* 4 − 2 = 6 − 3 = 7 − 3 = 9 − 5 = **Other number bonds** *Addition (missing addends)* 4 + ☐ = 6 2 + ☐ = 9 1 + ☐ = 5 3 + ☐ = 8 *Subtraction* 9 − 7 = 5 − 4 = 8 − 2 = 7 − 5 =		

Fingers	☐	Subvocalizing	☐	Counting all	☐
Counting on	☐	Step-counting	☐	Looking into space	☐
Reasoning from known facts	☐	Can't explain	☐		

For extra forms go to: http://education.emersonbabtie.continuumbooks.com

Number bonds: bonds of 10 and above to 100

- The bonds of ten are the pairs of numbers that add together to make ten.
- Bonds of ten facts underpin calculation throughout the number system.
- It is very important to spend sufficient time investigating the child's knowledge of bonds of ten and transference of knowledge of the bonds of ten to higher numbers.

Equipment: squared paper (1 cm²) and pencil.

Bonds of ten

Assessor writes the questions one at a time on squared paper. Ask the child to fill in the missing numbers.

Addition (missing addend)

$9 + \square = 10$ $8 + \square = 10$

$5 + \square = 10$ $3 + \square = 10$

$4 + \square = 10$

> - Can they give the answer quickly?
> - Do they count back?
> - Do they use fingers?
> - Do they use some other strategy?

Subtraction

$10 - 7 = \square$ $10 - 2 = \square$

$10 - 8 = \square$ $10 - 6 = \square$

> - Can they transfer their knowledge of the bonds of ten and apply it through the decades?
> - What strategies do they use?
> - Do they draw a number line?
> - Are they counting on or back or using their number bond knowledge? For example, if 6 + 4 = 10 then 16 + 4 = 20.

Bonds through the decades

If they can do the bonds of ten, investigate higher numbers. Write on squared paper.

Addition (missing addend)

$16 + \square = 20$ $24 + \square = 30$

$37 + \square = 40$ $52 + \square = 60$

Subtraction

$20 - 4 = \square$ $30 - 6 = \square$

$60 - 7 = \square$ $100 - 7 = \square$

Bonds of 100

If they can do the components of 10, investigate further and note strategies.

> - Are they using the facts of 10 to solve these?
> - Are they counting on or back?
> - Do they use a number line?

Addition (missing addends)

$90 + \square = 100$ $70 + \square = 100$

$30 + \square = 100$

Subtraction

$100 - 90 = \square$ $100 - 70 = \square$

$100 - 20 = \square$

Number bonds: bonds of 10 and above to 100

- The bonds of ten are the pairs of numbers that add together to make ten.
- Bonds of ten facts underpin calculation throughout the number system.
- It is very important to spend sufficient time investigating the child's knowledge of bonds of ten and transference of knowledge of the bonds of ten to higher numbers.

Questions	Star/tick	Comments
Written		
Bonds of ten		
Addition		
9 + ☐ = 10		
8 + ☐ = 10		
5 + ☐ = 10		
3 + ☐ = 10		
4 + ☐ = 10		
Subtraction		
10 – 7 = ☐		
10 – 2 = ☐		
10 – 8 = ☐		
10 – 6 = ☐		
Bonds through the decades		
Addition		
16 + ☐ = 20		
24 + ☐ = 30		
37 + ☐ = 40		
52 + ☐ = 60		
Subtraction		
20 – 4 = ☐		
30 – 6 = ☐		
60 – 7 = ☐		
100 – 7 = ☐		
Bonds of 100		
Addition		
90 + ☐ = 100		
70 + ☐ = 100		
30 + ☐ = 100		
Subtraction		
100 – 90 = ☐		
100 – 70 = ☐		
100 – 20 = ☐		

Fingers	☐	Subvocalizing	☐	Counting all	☐
Counting on	☐	Step-counting	☐	Looking into space	☐
Reasoning from known facts	☐	Can't explain	☐		

SECTION 3: PLACE VALUE

Equipment: 1 cm² squared paper and a pencil

Place value in calculations

It is essential to understand the concept of place value in order to calculate. In a multi-digit number the value of each digit depends on its position in the number.

This assessment checks that the child understands how the value of a digit varies according to its position in a number, and that they can apply this knowledge to calculations.

Ten plus a single digit

Add a single digit to ten to form the teen numbers.

e.g. $10 + 5 = 15$

Add a single digit to multiples of 10, e.g. $30 + 7 = 37$

Bridging

Bridging is a strategy using knowledge of the bonds of ten to calculate more efficiently than counting on in ones. Bridging involves using 10, or a multiple of 10, as a 'stepping stone' in a calculation.

e.g. $27 + 5 = (27 + 3) + 2 = 30 + 2 = 32$

Partitioning

This section checks the child's ability to partition, or separate, a number into hundreds, tens and units, and to use that knowledge for more efficient calculation.

e.g. 372 can be split into $300 + 70 + 2$

Place-value work

Understanding the value of digits in multi-digit numbers. Check that the child can do unit subtraction. In the sense used here, the unit quantity to be subtracted is the same as the units amount of the larger number.

e.g. $67 - 7 = 60$

Addition and subtraction of numbers involving 1s, 10s, 100s and 1000s is assessed to check understanding of place value.

Subtraction: doubles facts

Investigate whether the child can apply knowledge of the doubles facts.

e.g. Use the fact $7 + 7 = 14$ to reason that $14 - 7$ must equal 7.

Bridging back

Bridging back means using ten or a multiple of ten as a 'stepping stone' in a calculation.

e.g. $23 - 5 = (23 - 3) - 2 = 20 - 2 = 18$

Counting on for subtraction

This is often called the shopkeeper's method, or complementary addition.

The difference between two numbers is found by counting from the smaller number up to the larger number.

e.g. $73 - 65$

Start at 65 and count on in ones until you reach 73. The difference is the number counted on which is 8.

Counting on can also be combined with a bridging strategy.

Place value: ten plus a single digit

- Check that they understand that in the place-value system units are added to units, tens to tens, and hundreds to hundreds.
- Transference of knowledge of 'ten plus a single digit' to higher numbers.
- Ability to use the strategies based on bridging and partitioning.

Equipment: squared paper (1 cm²) and pencil.

Ten plus number (e.g. 10 + 5 = 15)
Write down for the child

10 + 4 = ☐   10 + 7 = ☐

> - Do they add the units to the units position?
> - Do they know the answer automatically or do they have to count from the beginning?
> - Do they count on from the first number?

Tens plus number (e.g. 40 + 7 = 47)

20 + 3 = ☐   30 + 5 = ☐
50 + 7 = ☐   80 + 4 = ☐

> - Can they explain their method or record their thinking?
> - Bridging: are they moving to the nearest tens number first?
> - Are they counting from the beginning? Are they making 10 first and then adding the rest to get to 12?
> - Are they using their fingers?

Bridging

The bridging strategy uses 10 or a multiple of 10 as a 'stepping stone' to the next number.
e.g. $7 + 5 = (7 + 3) + 2 = 10 + 2 = 12$
e.g. $37 + 5 = (37 + 3) + 2 = 40 + 2 = 42$

Bridging forwards through ten
Write the questions on the squared paper.

9 + 3 = ☐   8 + 4 = ☐
7 + 5 = ☐   6 + 5 = ☐

How did you do it?

Bridging through tens
Only if they are able to bridge through ten, investigate bridging through tens numbers.
Write the questions on the squared paper.

19 + 3 = ☐   28 + 4 = ☐
36 + 5 = ☐   87 + 6 = ☐

How did you do it?

> - Do they bridge to the next multiple of 10 or do they partition the tens and the units?
> - Bridging: $29 + 5 = (29 + 1) + 4 = 30 + 4 = 34$
> - Partitioning: $29 + 5 = (20 + 9) + 5 = 20 + 14 = 34$
> - Do they use a number line?

Place value: ten plus a single digit

- Check that they understand that in the place-value system units are added to units, tens to tens, and hundreds to hundreds.
- Transference of knowledge of 'ten plus a single digit' to higher numbers.
- Ability to use the strategies based on bridging and partitioning.

Questions	Star/tick	Comments
Ten plus number e.g. 10 + 5 = 15 10 + 4 = 10 + 7 =		
Tens plus number e.g. 40 + 7 = 47 20 + 3 = 30 + 5 = 50 + 7 = 80 + 4 =		
Bridging Through ten e.g. 7 + 5 = (7 + 3) + 2 = 10 + 2 = 12 9 + 3 = 8 + 4 = 7 + 5 = 6 + 5 =		
Through tens e.g. 37 + 5 = (37 + 3) + 2 = 40 + 2 = 42 19 + 3 = 28 + 4 = 36 + 5 = 87 + 6 =		

Fingers	☐	Subvocalizing	☐	Counting all	☐
Counting on	☐	Step-counting	☐	Looking into space	☐
Reasoning from known facts	☐	Can't explain	☐		

For extra forms go to: http://education.emersonbabtie.continuumbooks.com

Place value: the value of digits

- Investigate understanding of the value of the digits in the place-value system.
- Use of place-value knowledge to calculate.
- Ability to use the strategies based on partitioning.

Equipment: squared paper (1 cm²) and pencil.

Partitioning

Using place-value knowledge to partition numbers into tens and units to solve addition and subtraction.

Example: $35 + 62 = 30 + 5 + 60 + 2 = 90 + 7 = 97$

Write the questions on the squared paper and ask:

$21 + 34 = \square$ $\qquad$ $42 + 31 = \square$

How did you do it?

Unit subtraction

Check that the child can do unit subtraction. In the sense used here, the unit quantity to be subtracted is the same as the units amount of the larger number.

e.g. $27 - 7 = 20$

Write the questions one at a time on the squared paper.

$36 - 6 =$ $\qquad$ $48 - 8 =$
$53 - 3 =$ $\qquad$ $64 - 4 =$

> - Can they answer without calculating?
> - Do they count back in ones?

Adding 1s, 10s, 100s, 1000s

Write the questions below on the squared paper.

$172 + 10 =$ $\qquad$ $367 + 100 =$
$236 + 1 =$ $\qquad$ $1354 + 1000 =$
$462 + 1000 =$

> - Do they respond automatically, showing understanding of place value?
> - Do they need to count on?
> - Do they use their fingers?

Subtracting 1s, 10s, 100s, 1000s

Write the questions below on the squared paper.

$135 - 1 =$ $\qquad$ $142 - 10 =$
$356 - 100 =$ $\qquad$ $2473 - 1000 =$

Place value: the value of digits		
• Investigate understanding of the value of the digits in the place-value system.		
• Use of place-value knowledge to calculate.		
• Ability to use the strategies based on partitioning.		

Questions	Star/tick	Comments
Partitioning 21 + 34 = 42 + 31 =		
Unit subtraction Write on paper. Answers given orally. 36 – 6 = 48 – 8 = 53 – 3 = 64 – 4 =		
Adding 1s, 10s, 100s, 1000s Write on paper. Answers given orally. 172 + 10 = 367 + 100 = 236 + 1 = 1354 + 1000 = 462 + 1000 =		
Subtracting 1s, 10s, 100s, 1000s Write on paper. Answers given orally. 135 – 1 = 142 – 10 = 356 – 100 = 2473 – 1000 =		

Fingers	☐	Subvocalizing	☐	Counting all	☐
Counting on	☐	Step-counting	☐	Looking into space	☐
Reasoning from known facts	☐	Can't explain	☐		

Place value: subtraction strategies

- Investigate the application of calculation strategies: doubles, bridging back, counting up (complementary addition).

Equipment: squared paper (1 cm²) and pencil.

Doubles subtraction
Applying doubles and near doubles facts.

> - Do they recognize number combinations that are part of the doubles patterns and use these?
> - Do they count back in ones?
> - Do they use a number line?
> - Do they count on?

Write these down on the squared paper. Ask:
How did you do that?
    The child answers orally.

$14 - 7 =$ $18 - 9 =$
$12 - 6 =$ $16 - 8 =$

> - Can they bridge back through tens numbers? Example: $23 - 5 = (23 - 3) - 2 = 20 - 2 = 18$
> - Can they explain or record their thinking?
> - Do they count back in ones?
> - Do they draw a number line?
> - Are they are using a mental number line? (Evidence for this may be slight movement of the lips, or looking upwards.)

Subtracting back (bridging back)
Using ten or a multiple of ten as a 'stepping stone' in a calculation.
    e.g. $13 - 8 = (13 - 3) - 5 = 5$

Write these down on the squared paper. Ask: *How did you do that?*
    The child answers orally.

$23 - 4 =$ $52 - 5 =$
$63 - 5 =$ $73 - 6 =$

Counting up (complementary addition or the shopkeeper's method)
The difference between two numbers is found by counting from the smaller number up to the larger number in ones or in groups.

$73 - 65 =$ $26 - 17 =$
$52 - 37 =$

> - Are they counting up from the smaller number in ones?
> - Do they bridge back?
> - Do they draw a number line or solve it mentally?
> - Do they solve it by rewriting formally?

Example:
$27 - 15 = 12$

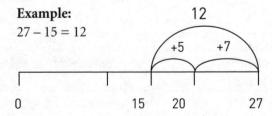

Place value: subtraction strategies

- Investigate the application of calculation strategies: doubles, bridging back, counting up (complementary addition).

Questions	Star/tick	Comments
Write these down on the squared paper. Answers given orally. **Doubles subtraction** $14 - 7 =$ $18 - 9 =$ $12 - 6 =$ $16 - 8 =$		
Subtracting back (bridging back) e.g. $23 - 5 = (23 - 3) - 2 = 20 - 2 = 18$ Write these down on the squared paper: $23 - 4 =$ $52 - 5 =$ $63 - 5 =$ $73 - 6 =$		
Counting on (complementary addition, also called the shopkeeper's method) $73 - 65 =$ $26 - 17 =$ $52 - 37 =$ $27 - 15 =$		

Fingers	☐	Subvocalizing	☐	Counting all	☐
Counting on	☐	Step-counting	☐	Looking into space	☐
Reasoning from known facts	☐	Can't explain	☐		

End of Place value section: Pause for a brief chat. Choosing a reward sticker can be helpful.

For extra forms go to: http://education.emersonbabtie.continuumbooks.com

SECTION 4: MULTIPLICATION AND DIVISION

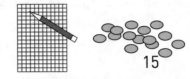

Equipment: pencil, squared paper (1 cm²), 15 counters (same colour).

Concepts

Multiplication encompasses two ideas – repeated addition and the area model. Children who are struggling with maths can be confused by the area model so this assessment only investigates multiplication as repeated addition.

Division is the inverse of multiplication. Check if the child knows this.

The language of tables

Children who do not understand the concept of multiplication may be confused by the language of multiplication. They do not understand the difference between 5 times 3 and 3 times 5.* It is clearer to say 5 threes or 3 fives. However, the assessor should use the words that the child is familiar with. Write 2×3 and ask the child to read it. Note what language they use.

Reasoning strategies

Find out if the child knows any tables off by heart.

Find out if the child is using any reasoning strategies to work out tables they do not know. Some common strategies are as follows.

- **Step-counting:** To calculate 4×5 step-count: 5, 10, 15, 20.
- **Commutativity principle:** If they know that $8 \times 5 = 40$ they know that $5 \times 8 = 40$.
- **Work from a known fact:** If they know that $5 \times 3 = 15$ then 6 threes must be one more three so that $6 \times 3 = 18$.
- **Halving:** The child needs to understand that 5 is half of 10. Then they can derive 5 times a number by finding half of 10 times the number. Example: If $10 \times 4 = 40$, then 5×4 must be half of 40.

Counter demonstration

Check whether the child understands the concept of multiplication by asking them to demonstrate using counters. Example: 3 fives would be 3 groups with five in each group compared to 5 threes where there are 5 groups of three.

Division

The concept of division involves either grouping or sharing a quantity.

Many children do not realize that division is the inverse of multiplication. Find out how they think about division and whether they are able to use their knowledge of tables to solve division questions.

---

* Because multiplication is a commutative operation, the result of multiplying 5 times 3 or 3 times 5 will be the same. The point made here is that children need to understand the concept that is being expressed. Example: 5 children with 3 balloons each is different to 3 children with 5 balloons each. While the total number of balloons is 15 in both cases, the number of children varies.

Multiplication tables

- Check which tables the child knows.
- Find out which words they use to talk about multiplication.

Equipment: squared paper (1 cm²) and pencil.

The language of tables and reasoning ability

Which tables have you learnt at school?
Which tables do you know?

> Note the language the child uses. They may say:
> - 2 times 3
> - 2 threes
> - 2 lots of 3
> - 2 groups of three.
>
> During the assessment use the child's choice of language to avoid confusion.

Explore the child's knowledge and reasoning. Write the question and each time say:
Read it to me. Can you write the answer?

After the child has written the answer ask:
How did you do that?

$2 \times 3 =$
$6 \times 2 =$
$10 \times 3 =$
$5 \times 3 =$
$6 \times 3 =$

> Examples of possible responses from the child:
> - I just know it.
> - I know $5 \times 2 = 10$ so 6×2 must be 2 more.
> - I know $6 + 6$ and that is what 2×6 means.
> - I counted in 2s and used my fingers to count 6 twos.
> - I know 3 tens are 30 so 10 threes are 30.
> - I know 10×3 is 30 so 5×3 is half of that so it is 15.
> - Half of 30 is 15.

If they know the easy tables (2s, 5s, 10s), check a harder even-number table such as the 8 times table. If they say they do not know the 8s, ask them to have a look and see if they can have a go.

Write the question and ask: *Read it to me. Can you write the answer?*
$5 \times 8 =$

> - Do they know the answer only by reciting it from the beginning?
> - Do they solve 5×8 by reverting to 5x table facts?
> - Do they reason from 10×8 to 5×8 by halving?
> - Do they try to step-count in 8s?
> - Do they understand the concept of thinking in groups of 8?

If they are successful then find out if they can reason from the known fact of 5×8:
If $5 \times 8 = 40$ then what would 6×8 be?

> - Are they able to get to 6×8 from 5×8?
> - Do they add 8 to 40 with ease or do they have to count on in ones?

Multiplication tables
• Check which tables the child knows.
• Find out which words they use to talk about multiplication.

Questions	Star/tick	Comments
The language of tables and reasoning ability 2 × 3 Note if they say '2 times 3' or '2 threes'. 6 × 2 = 10 × 3 = 5 × 3 = 6 × 3 = 5 × 8 = 6 × 8 =		

Fingers	☐	Subvocalizing	☐	Counting all	☐
Counting on	☐	Step-counting	☐	Looking into space	☐
Reasoning from known facts	☐	Can't explain	☐		

Multiplication: counter demonstration

- Investigate whether the child understands what the tables represent.

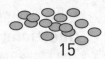

15

Equipment: 15 counters (all the same colour).

Counter demonstration

Give the child 15 counters and ask them to show you '3 × 5'.
Use the language they used in the previous section. If the child
did not show a preference use the form '3 fives'.

EITHER *Show me 3 times 5.* OR *Show me 3 fives.*

> - Any arrangement that
>   clearly shows there are
>   3 groups with five in each
>   group is acceptable.

If they have no idea, even with a little prompting, demonstrate
with 2 twos (not giving the idea away completely). Then ask
them to show you 3 twos by setting out counters in groups.

Show me 3 twos with these counters. (Give them
6 counters.)

Now can you show me 2 threes?

> - Are they able to talk about
>   what they can see?

Here I have got 2 counters.
Assessor puts out counters.

And here I have got another 2 counters.
Puts out 2 more.
Say *I can see 2 twos.*
Remove the counters.

Give the child a pile of 10 counters.
Can you show me 3 twos?
Child puts them out.

If child puts out this pattern do not tell
them that it is incorrect. Note it down.

> - If children put out 2 threes
>   instead of 3 twos it shows
>   they may know the answer
>   but not fully understand
>   what it means.

What did you make?
I made 3 twos.
Yes, you made 3 twos. Put the counters back in the pile.

Now can you make 2 threes?
Child makes 2 threes.

Multiplication: counter demonstration

- Investigate whether the child understands what the tables represent.

Questions	Star/tick	Comments
Counter demonstration Give pupil 15 counters and ask them to show you '3 × 5'. Use the language they used in the previous section. i.e. EITHER: *Show me 3 times 5.* OR *Show me 3 fives.* Give the child 10 counters. Ask them to demonstrate 3 twos. Ask them to demonstrate 2 threes.		

Fingers	☐	Subvocalizing	☐	Counting all	☐
Counting on	☐	Step-counting	☐	Looking into space	☐
Reasoning from known facts	☐	Can't explain	☐		

Division

- Check automatic recall of division facts, and the use of vocabulary associated with division.
- Find out how the child solves division problems.
- Can they use the group concept correctly or do they always revert to sharing.

Equipment: squared paper (1 cm²) and pencil.

Oral questions

Give some oral examples linked to multiplication:

How many twos make 8?
    Child answers [4].

How did you do that?

How many threes do you need to build 15?
    Child answers [5].

How did you do that?

What is 30 divided by 5?
    If they cannot understand the term 'divided by' ask: *How many 5s in 30?*

> Possible responses:
> - I know it.
> - I know that 4 twos are 8 (multiplication).
> - I counted 2, 4, 6, 8 (step-counting).
> - I know there are 4 twos in 8 (the most sophisticated response).

> Possible responses:
> - I know 5 threes are 15.
> - I know 3 fives are 15.
> - You need 5 groups of 3 to build 15.

> - Do they use their fingers?
> - Do they need to draw a diagram?
> - Do they need to draw tally marks?

Written questions

Write the following questions one at a time on squared paper.

Can you write the answer?

$10 \div 2 =$

$20 \div 5 =$

$12 \div 4 =$

$42 \div 6 =$

Division

- Check automatic recall of division facts, and the use of vocabulary associated with division.
- Find out how the child solves division problems.
- Can they use the group concept correctly or do they always revert to sharing.

Questions	Star/tick	Comments
Division **Oral** *How many twos make 8?* *How many threes do you need to build 15?* *What is 30 divided by 5?* (If they cannot understand the term 'divided by' say: *How many 5s in 30?*) **Written questions** Ask the pupil to write the answer. $10 \div 2 =$ $20 \div 5 =$ $12 \div 4 =$ $42 \div 6 =$		

Fingers	☐	Subvocalizing	☐	Counting all	☐
Counting on	☐	Step-counting	☐	Looking into space	☐
Reasoning from known facts	☐	Can't explain	☐		

For extra forms go to: http://education.emersonbabtie.continuumbooks.com

SECTION 5: WORD PROBLEMS

Equipment: squared paper (1 cm²) and pencil.

Classification of word problems

Children need to apply their knowledge of the four arithmetical operations to word problems by selecting the appropriate operation and performing the calculation.

Word problems can be classified into the following categories:

- combine, change and compare for addition and subtraction
- repeated addition and the array and area models for multiplication
- grouping and sharing models for division.

Language and concept

Children need to be able to understand the language of word problems. They need to be clear about what the question is asking and the concept involved in order to work out which arithmetical operation to use. Sometimes children are taught to indentify 'trigger' words to help them choose an arithmetical operation. However trigger words can be misleading. Example: 'Altogether' may require addition, multiplication or division.

I have 3 apples and 2 pears. How many pieces of fruit do I have altogether? (Addition)

There are four horses. How many legs are there altogether? (Multiplication)

24 children are put into teams of 3. How many teams are there altogether? (Division)

Word problems: addition, multiplication and subtraction

- Find out if the child can understand word problems and use the appropriate arithmetical operation to solve them.
- Keep the wording very simple to create a straightforward word problem of a particular type.

Equipment: 1 cm² squared paper and a pencil.

Word problems: addition, multiplication and subtraction

The assessor writes the problem as briefly as possible.

In each case ask the child: *Can you read this to me?* (If they cannot read, the assessor reads the question to them.) Ask the child if they can explain how they solved the problem.

> - Does the child draw to solve the problems before being asked to do so?
> - If a child gives an incorrect answer, do not tell them they are incorrect but suggest they do a drawing.
> - Does the child self-correct after drawing?

a. Addition problem: combine

Jon had 6 sweets. Mum gave him 3 more.
> *How many sweets does Jon have?*
> Child answers [9 sweets].
> *How did you do that?*

b. Multiplication problem: repeated addition

There are 4 ponds. There are 2 ducks on each pond.
> The assessor writes:
> There are 4 ponds. 2 ducks on each pond.
> *Can you read that to me?*

If they cannot read it, read it to them.
> *How many ducks are there?*
> Child says [8 ducks].
> *How did you do that? Can you draw a picture of this? I just want a quick drawing; this is not an art lesson.*

> - Do they know their multiplication tables?
> - Do they use repeated addition?
> - Do they step-count?

Ask the child to explain their drawing.
> *Can you write this in numbers?*
> (You want the child to write the sum in numbers, e.g. 4 × 2 = 8.)

> Possible responses: I just know it.
> *How did you get your answer?*
> 2, 4, 6, 8 (counting in 2s)

c. Subtraction problem: change

There were 7 ducks on a pond. A gun made a bang. 3 ducks flew away. How many ducks are still on the pond?
> Assessor writes: 7 ducks on a pond. 3 ducks flew away.
> *How many ducks are there now?*
> *How did you do that?*
> *Can you write this in numbers?* (You want a number sentence.)

Word problems: addition, multiplication and subtraction

- Find out if the child can understand word problems and use the appropriate arithmetical operation to solve them.
- Keep the wording very simple to create a straightforward word problem of a particular type.

Questions	Star/tick	Comments
Word problems		
a. Jon had 6 sweets. Mum gave him 3 more. How many sweets does Jon have?		
b. There are 4 ponds. 2 ducks on each pond. How many ducks are there?		
c. 7 ducks on a pond. A gun made a bang. 3 ducks flew away. How many ducks are still on the pond?		

Fingers	☐	Subvocalizing	☐	Counting all	☐
Counting on	☐	Step-counting	☐	Looking into space	☐
Reasoning from known facts	☐	Can't explain	☐		

Word problems: division

Grouping or sharing word problems

- Find out if the child can understand division word problems and solve them by using the concept of grouping or sharing.
- Keep the wording very simple to create a straightforward word problem.

Equipment: 1 cm² squared paper and a pencil.

Word problems: division

Even if the pupil cannot solve a formal division problem, see if they can solve a word-based problem involving grouping or sharing.

Ask the child to solve the problem. Do not help by telling them to put quantities into groups, or to share them.

The assessor writes the problem as briefly as possible.

In each case ask the child: *Can you read this to me?* (If they cannot read, the assessor reads the question to them.) Ask the child if they can explain how they solved the problem.

The grouping concept of division:

12 girls are told to get into teams with 3 in each team.

How many teams will there be?

Assessor writes: 12 girls. 3 girls in each team.

How many teams will there be?

When the child has responded ask:

How did you do that?

Can you write this in numbers?

- Can they derive the answer from multiplication knowledge?
- Note whether they draw to try to solve the problem.
- Do they step-count?
- Are they able to produce the division sign?

(You want the child to write: 12 ÷ 3 = 4)

The sharing concept of division:

You have 24 apples to put into bags. You have 6 bags.

How many apples in each bag?

Assessor writes: 24 apples. 6 bags.

How many apples in each bag?

When the child has responded ask:

How did you do that?

Can you write this in numbers?

(You want the child to write the sum in numbers, e.g. 24 ÷ 6 = 4.)

Word problems: division
Grouping or sharing word problems
- Find out if the child can understand division word problems and solve them by using the concept of grouping or sharing.
- Keep the wording very simple to create a straightforward word problem.

Questions	Star/tick	Comments
Division by grouping 12 girls are told to get into teams with 3 in each team. How many teams will there be?		
Division by sharing You have 24 apples to put into bags. You have 6 bags. How many apples in each bag?		

Fingers	☐	Subvocalizing	☐	Counting all	☐
Counting on	☐	Step-counting	☐	Looking into space	☐
Reasoning from known facts	☐	Can't explain	☐		

End of Word problems section: Pause for a brief chat. Choosing a reward sticker can be helpful.

© Jane Emerson and Patricia Babtie 2010. *The Dyscalculia Assessment.*
For extra forms go to: http://education.emersonbabtie.continuumbooks.com

SECTION 6: FORMAL WRITTEN NUMERACY

Equipment: squared paper (1 cm²) and pencil

Standard algorithms

The formal written numeracy section investigates how the child performs calculations using standard algorithms – the step-by-step procedures used for calculating with multi-digit numbers. The steps need to be done in a specific order.

If their reasoning skills are poor, children with weak numeracy skills may prefer to use these standard procedures. However, they may be following a procedure without understanding the maths concepts behind it. If they have a poor memory they may muddle up the sequence of steps, which will lead to errors.

Place value

In order to use formal written methods effectively, children need to understand the place-value system and be able to apply the principle of exchange. They need to be able to decompose numbers. They need to carry out the steps of the procedure in the correct order.

Children who use formal written methods in a mechanical way may not be able to do required exchanges between place-value columns.

Formal written numeracy: addition and subtraction

- Investigate how the child performs written maths problems.
- Observe the order in which the steps of the calculation are carried out.
- Note if they are able to apply the principle of exchange correctly.

Equipment: squared paper (1 cm²) and pencil.

Addition

Assessor writes:

Add 23 and 45.

Assessor says: *Show me how you would solve this.*

> - Note responses when the problem does not require an exchange as opposed to when it does and record errors.
> - Supply squared paper.

The child may solve it by partitioning, e.g. 2 3 + 4 5 = (20 + 40) + (3 + 5) = 68.

If they solve the first question using partitioning, ask them to add 42 and 36 and write them in columns and work it out. (If they do not know what columns are, the teacher sets it out for them and asks them to solve it.)

42
36 +

What did you add?

The expected response from the child is: 'I added 42 and 36'.

> If the child says, 'I added 4 and 3 and 2 and 6' they may not understand that they are adding 42 and 36. They may be just trying to remember a procedure they have been taught.

The assessor writes the following sums and asks the child to solve them. These questions assess the child's ability to exchange.

35	105	4 067
47 +	657 +	3 425 +

Next, ask the child to write the numbers below as a formal addition. The assessor dictates the numbers.

Write these numbers in columns: 67 + 532 + 4. Can you add them all together?

> - Are they confused about decomposing numbers and carrying over to another place-value column?
> - Are they unclear about where to put the carried digits?

Subtraction

Investigate written subtraction.

The assessor writes down the questions one at a time.

> Can the child use zero appropriately?

27	64	134	1 003
13 −	17 −	65 −	539 −

Formal written numeracy: addition and subtraction

- Investigate how the child performs written maths problems.
- Observe the order in which the steps of the calculation are carried out.
- Note if they are able to apply the principle of exchange correctly.

Questions	Star/tick	Comments
Addition Add 23 and 45. $\quad$ 42 $\quad$ 36 + $\quad$ 35 $\quad$ 47 + $\quad$ 105 $\quad$ 657 + 4 067 3 425 + *Write these numbers in columns: 67 + 532 + 4. Can you add them?* **Subtraction** Write these on squared paper. $\quad$ 27 $\quad$ 13 – $\quad$ 64 $\quad$ 17 – $\quad$ 134 $\quad$ 65 – 1 003 $\quad$ 539 –		

Fingers	☐	Subvocalizing	☐	Counting all	☐
Counting on	☐	Step-counting	☐	Looking into space	☐
Reasoning from known facts	☐	Can't explain	☐		

Formal written numeracy: multiplication

- Check understanding of multiplication.
- Find out if they can use standard written algorithms.
- Check correct use of zero as a place holder.
- Observe the order in which procedures are carried out.

Equipment: squared paper (1 cm²) and pencil.

Multiplication

I want you to do some multiplication.
Assessor writes down:

$$\begin{array}{r} 12 \\ 6 \times \\ \hline \end{array}$$

Do you know what 12 sixes are?
    If the child is unable to do this, help them by asking:
    Do you know what 10 sixes are? Does that help you to work out 12 sixes?

 Stop the assessment at this point if the child is unable to work out 12 × 6.

If the child is successful assessor writes down:

Do you know what 13 sixes are?   13
    How did you do that?   6 ×
                                        ───

Assessor writes down the following questions one at a time.
Can you do these for me now?

$$\begin{array}{r} 10 \\ 8 \times \\ \hline \end{array} \qquad \begin{array}{r} 5 \\ 8 \times \\ \hline \end{array} \qquad \begin{array}{r} 15 \\ 8 \times \\ \hline \end{array}$$

How did you work out 15 eights?

Long multiplication

Assessor writes the following questions one at a time in the standard form.

$$\begin{array}{r} 23 \\ 10 \times \\ \hline \end{array} \qquad \begin{array}{r} 23 \\ 15 \times \\ \hline \end{array} \qquad \begin{array}{r} 27 \\ 4 \times \\ \hline \end{array}$$

Can you do these for me now?
How did you do that?

- What methods have they been taught at school?
- Do they have any rote knowledge?
- Do they use the standard algorithm?
- Do they use a taught strategy such as a Simple Box Method?

  Simple Box Method

×	10	5
20	200	100
3	30	15

23 × 15 = 200 + 100 + 30 + 15
        = 300 + 45
        = 345

- Do they relate 13 × 6 to the tables or to 12 sixes?
- Or do they treat it as a completely new problem? Do they realize that the answer to 13 × 6 is going to be one more six than 12 × 6 or three more sixes than 10 × 6?

- Do they derive 5 × 8 from halving 10 × 8?
- Do they solve 15 × 8 from the previous items, or treat it as a new problem?

- How do they record the exchanges where units are carried into the tens column?

Formal written numeracy: multiplication

- Check understanding of multiplication and division.
- Find out if they can use standard written algorithms.
- Check correct use of zero as a place holder.
- Observe the order in which procedures are carried out.

Questions	Star/tick	Comments
Multiplication		
12 6 ×		
13 6 ×		
10 8 ×		
5 8 ×		
15 8 ×		
Long multiplication		
23 10 ×		
23 15 ×		
27 4 ×		

Fingers	☐	Subvocalizing	☐	Counting all	☐
Counting on	☐	Step-counting	☐	Looking into space	☐
Reasoning from known facts	☐	Can't explain	☐		

Formal written numeracy: division

- Investigate their understanding of division and if they relate it to multiplication.
- Check their understanding of remainders if appropriate.
- Observe the order in which procedures are carried out.

Equipment: squared paper (1 cm²) and pencil.

Division

Ask the child to solve the following questions. Allow them to write them down in the standard form if they want to do so.

Assessor writes down the following questions one at a time:

$45 \div 5$

$78 \div 2$

Can you do these for me?
After each one ask: *How did you do that?*

$140 \div 10$

$132 \div 10$

$4\,500 \div 100$

- Do they use a learnt 'recipe'? Do they solve it with understanding?
- Do they write out 4500 ÷ 100 as a standard written division?
- Are they able to derive the answer from their understanding that 14 × 10 or 10 × 14 = 140, therefore there must be 14 tens in 140?

Written division

Write these questions down for the child one at a time as a standard division algorithm. Each time ask: *Can you do these for me? How did you do it?*

$95 \div 5$

$6\overline{)25}$

$7\overline{)436}$

- Do they solve 95 ÷ 5 by relating it to the 5 times table?
- Has the child understood that the question is asking how many fives there are in 95?
- Do they solve it formally by setting it out as a short division sum $5\overline{)95}$?
- Do they understand the concept of remainders?
- If they get it right with remainders, can they tell you what their answer means? Can they tell you what an answer with a remainder means?
- Can they tell you that there are 4 sixes in 25 with one left over?

Formal written numeracy: division

- Investigate their understanding of division and whether they relate it to multiplication.
- Check their understanding of remainders if appropriate.
- Observe the order in which procedures are carried out.

Questions	Star/tick	Comments
Division		
45 ÷ 5 78 ÷ 2		
140 divided by 10 *132 divided by 10* *4 500 divided by 100*		
Written division 95 ÷ 5		
With remainders: 6⟌25 7⟌436		

Fingers	☐	Subvocalizing	☐	Counting all	☐
Counting on	☐	Step-counting	☐	Looking into space	☐
Reasoning from known facts	☐	Can't explain	☐		

End of Dyscalculia Assessment: Allow the child to choose a reward sticker.

© Jane Emerson and Patricia Babtie 2010. *The Dyscalculia Assessment.*
For extra forms go to: http://education.emersonbabtie.continuumbooks.com

Interpreting the assessment

This chapter discusses why errors may have occurred and suggests how to remediate them.

This chapter covers the following:

Initial discussion

General observations

1. Anxiety levels Many children struggling with maths have some level of anxiety. This may be evident from their appearance or behaviour. They will need extra reassurance and encouragement.

   If you found signs of significant levels of anxiety, consider referring the child to a school counsellor or their family doctor, especially if you have been unable to conduct the assessment. Sometimes a young child may refuse to do an assessment and this may have been interpreted as defiance when in fact it is caused by severe maths anxiety, making it impossible for the child to do any maths. This is, however, a rare occurrence if the assessor is sufficiently encouraging so that the child understands that the assessment is not a test but to see what they can do in maths.

> **Teaching plan: *note anxiety level***
> In order to overcome initial anxiety, it is essential that the child experiences complete success in the initial stages of the teaching intervention. Anxious children will need teaching to start at a level where they can do all the maths correctly and confidently. This may mean starting at a point just before the child has made an error. They will also need extra reassurance and encouragement. Some children may need to be rewarded with a sticker or other token for each item they attempt in the investigation or in subsequent lessons.

2. Attention levels If the child is unable to remain seated on the chair, consider using a different kind of chair. For instance, a Trip Trap chair promotes good posture and enables the child to be pushed up closely to the table, ensuring they remain seated. Remember to keep the table and even the room completely clear of unnecessary objects to reduce distractions.

> **Teaching plan:** *impulsivity and short attention span*
>
> In order to enable a child with a short attention span to remain focused, keep the activities short. Gradually, over several sessions, increase the length of the activities within each session. Initially, some children may need to do something different every 5 or 10 minutes so be prepared to work on several different things in each session. However if a child becomes fascinated by one activity allow them to continue a little longer.
>
> It is important to train impulsive children that there is a plan for the lesson and that the teacher is in charge of the plan. If the child loses interest, shorten the time spent on that activity without letting them know that they have had an influence on your decision.
>
> Give clear instructions without using any pleasantries such as 'please' as this gives the child the idea you are asking if they will comply. They will feel more secure if short, clear instructions are delivered in a friendly way.

Attitudes to school and maths

1. How is their school work in general? Remember to reconsider the question: 'Is there a discrepancy between their other school work and their maths?' If there is a discrepancy it indicates it is likely that the child has a specific maths difficulty which should be intensively addressed. If there is no discrepancy, intervention specialists should formulate a combined plan to cover the child's needs in all areas of difficulty. Whoever is teaching the child should be fully aware of the child's reading age levels and bear in mind how this will affect reading in maths lessons. The child will need help learning to read and understand maths words and to follow mathematical instructions in word problems.

2. How is their maths in particular? Answers to this question will give the assessor a feel for the child's attitude to maths. If the child has a positive attitude this may mean that the pace of the lessons can be quicker. However, many children with maths difficulties have a negative attitude to the subject and fear it. Some may become tearful.

Be constantly aware of, and use, all opportunities for promoting and encouraging a positive attitude to maths for children with low numeracy. Games are a good way to foster a positive attitude to maths. The games in Chapter 6 are designed to practise specific areas of numeracy and to encourage children to talk about what they are doing.

> **Teaching plan:** *foster a positive attitude to maths*
>
> Maths games are a very effective way of encouraging children to enjoy maths. However, losing a game can be traumatic for children with low self-esteem. Choose games where the teacher can control the outcome, such as 'pairs' games, if a particular child is a poor loser.
>
> If a child does not even want to play a game, or to receive stickers, try doing some maths in a different location such as in the playground or in the garden. Each teaching session should always end with a fun activity or game to end the session on a positive note that the child will remember.

What do you like doing and what don't you like doing in maths? Some children enjoy counting because they have good memories but may dislike work with shapes because they may have a visual perceptual difficulty. Others may hate counting because they have a sequential memory weakness but enjoy work with shapes because they have good visual perceptual abilities. Some children find reasoning about numbers very hard and will avoid talking about how they reached their answers.

> **Teaching plan:** *simplify tasks, start from a point of success*
> Try to plan the lesson for each child with a variety of activities to address aspects of maths that the child finds easy followed by tasks that they find more difficult or enjoy less. In this way the lesson will be balanced between things children like doing and things they dislike doing. If it becomes apparent that the child hates doing certain things, keep a careful note to introduce the activity through a game or fun activity. If a child hates working with shapes and patterns, consider a referral to an occupational therapist or an orthoptist and behavioural optometrist.[1] Try to simplify the task to find a baseline point of success and work slowly forward from there. If a child cannot solve missing addends, such as 2 + ? = 4, produce the simplest example of this type possible to make sure the child experiences success.

Maths investigation

Section 1: Number sense and counting

This section analyses the child's ability
- to sequence numbers
- to understand the tens based structure of the number system
- to read and write numbers.

Subitizing

Subitizing is an innate skill that most young children have. Children should be able to recognize and say the correct number word for up to 4 objects without counting when these are randomly scattered. If the child cannot state accurately how many counters there are without counting, this indicates very poor pattern recognition skills.

> **Teaching plan:** *subitizing; recognizing dice patterns*
> Work on recognizing small quantities of items, without counting. Put out a few counters (up to 4). Let the child look at them for one or two seconds and then cover the counters with a piece of A4 paper. Ask the child to say how many items they saw before they were covered up. Remove the piece of paper and ask the child to check their guess against the actual number of objects now visible. In this way children build up their knowledge and feel for very small quantities and learn to recognize the quantities involved without counting. After this continue the development of subitizing through the use of dot patterns, gradually increasing the size of the numbers.
>
> Formally teach the conventional 1–6 dice patterns one by one using counters of the same colour. Get the child to build each pattern while encouraging them to talk about what they are doing and about the differences between each number that they build. (See Chapter 6 for further games and activities for teaching dot patterns.)
>
> Informally, play dice games with the children. There are many suitable games available from toy shops such as Ludo, Around the World and Monopoly. The layout of Snakes and Ladders can be confusing for some children so give plenty of guidance as necessary.

Estimating

Between 5 and 10 items A close estimate of the actual number is acceptable. A more serious error of judgement, such as estimating 3 as 10, suggests a lack of sense of number and a poor awareness of quantities.

Check that the child can synchronize moving the counters and saying number words. If they cannot do this accurately, possible causes include lack of one-to-one correspondence, or impulsivity.

> ### Teaching plan: *estimating; counting accurately 5–10*
>
> Play an estimating game with 5 to 10 counters. This involves showing the child up to ten items for two to three seconds before covering them with a piece of A4 paper. Let the child guess how many they think are under the paper. Write down the number guessed. Remove the piece of paper and let the child count the number of objects into a line. Make sure the child synchronizes moving the counters with saying the number words.
>
> If the child lacks one-to-one correspondence, or is impulsive, train them to practise touching or moving the objects as they say the number words. This will slow them down which will improve their concentration and reduce impulsivity and inaccuracy. If they are unable to count accurately touching the counters and saying the numbers, count items with them. The child should set the pace and the teacher should match their speed to the child's speed.
>
> If the child is consistently miscounting, they will not be building up a stable sense of number and will need more guided practice working with the teacher. A good way of practising this skill is to do activities and games with the dot patterns discussed on page 135.

Between 10 and 20 items Note how realistic the guess is and how it compares with the previous estimate (between 5 and 10). If the child moves or touches the counters this is a positive sign of early strategy development.

> ### Teaching plan: *estimating; counting accurately 10–20; tens structure*
>
> Play the estimating game described above with up to 20 counters. Instructions for the Estimating Game, a competitive version of this game, are available in Chapter 6 (page 139).
>
> The way that the child puts out the counters and counts them will indicate whether they understand that the number system is a tens-based system. Make sure that the child leaves a gap after each group of ten counters to emphasize the tens-based nature of the number system. Problems may occur when the child places counters in a line. The child may put 9 instead of 10 counters before leaving a gap. Do not correct this but observe whether they notice this when they check it.
>
> The best way to demonstrate the tens structure is to place counters on a structured number track that clearly shows the end of each group of ten. The game Caterpillar Tracks (page 140) emphasizes the tens structure.

'-teen' numbers (13–19) Many children have particular problems with the -teen numbers so it is very important to investigate at least two numbers in the -teens, especially 13 and 15.

Example: Putting out 14 counters

Incorrect ⊙⊙⊙⊙⊙⊙⊙⊙⊙ ⊙⊙⊙⊙⊙

Correct ⊙⊙⊙⊙⊙⊙⊙⊙⊙⊙ ⊙⊙⊙⊙

When they have put out 10 and then some more counters, can they continue to count on from 10, or do they have to go back to the beginning and count all the counters?

Note pronunciation of the '-teen' numbers. The numbers 13 and 15 can cause particular confusion. (Some children may say 'threeteen' and 'fiveteen'.)

More than 20 items Note how accurate the estimation is.
When the child has put out groups of tens they should understand what these mean.

Example: Putting out 23

The child should be able to say there are two lines of tens and three more, or there are 20 and three more, or say 23. When asked how they know there are 23, can they explain this as two groups of 10 and 3 more?

Note if the child had to count in ones from the beginning again.

If they have miscounted, did they omit one or more numbers? Or did they fail to synchronize the number names with the counters? This indicates a lack of one-to-one correspondence skills.

> ### Teaching plan: *pronunciation of '-teen' and '-ty' endings; estimating larger quantities; counting larger numbers accurately; tens structure*
>
> If their pronunciation is unclear, ask the child to write the number down. If they say thirty but write 13, record this as correct but note the oral confusion and include it in the report and the teaching plan. Children will need careful training to distinguish between the spoken '-teen' and the '-ty' numbers. The teacher should exaggerate the difference and teach the child to do the same.
>
> Spending sufficient time allowing the child to develop an accurate and consistent counting strategy is important in laying down good foundations. They need practice at working with varying quantities of counters and placing them in lines, leaving a space between each group of ten counters. Play the Estimating Game (page 139).

Oral counting

Children should be able to count fluently without undue hesitation and pauses. If they are unable to do this they will need explicit instruction as suggested above.

Counting forwards in ones The child should be able to count forwards, known as counting on, from any number. Some children may have to go back and start from one. Children may omit numbers, especially in the teens, and may get stuck at a crossover point. A crossover point occurs when numbers change from one decade to another such as moving from twenties to thirties as in 28, 29, **30**, 31, 32. Dyscalculic children may say 28, 29, **20**, 21, 22 or show other confusions such as 'twenty-nine' followed by 'twenty-ten'. Some may have no idea that the thirties follow the twenties and so on.

Counting backwards in ones Counting backwards will be difficult for the child with a poor sense of numerical order. This may be caused by a weak auditory sequential memory. (This may mean that the child needs to be referred to an educational psychologist for further investigation of their memory.) Errors may include omitting numbers, or getting stuck at crossover points so they get stuck in a 'loop' (e.g. saying … 33, 32, 31, 30, 39, 38, 37 …). They may count forwards to check the next number. For example, counting back from 15, they may think 12, 13, 14, before saying 14. Indications of this may be evident from subtle use of the fingers, or whispering under their breath, known as subvocalizing.

Step-counting Counting forwards in tens: The child may count 70, 80, 90, 20. This indicates auditory confusion between '-teen' and '-ty' numbers (numbers whose names end in '-ty', e.g. twenty, thirty), confusing ninety with nineteen.

When counting in 10s beyond 100, the child may say: 90, 100, 200, 300. This indicates that the child does not understand how the number system is structured.

Counting forwards in fives: Difficulties counting in fives may indicate a difficulty in remembering the sequence of counting in fives or may indicate a lack of awareness that five is the halfway point in each decade.

Counting forwards in twos: Hesitation when counting in twos may indicate that the child is counting every alternate number under their breath. They say 2, 4, 6, 8 … but are thinking **2**, 3, **4**, 5, **6** … The process of step-counting has not become automatic.

Teaching plan: *oral counting; counting forwards; counting backwards; sequencing, step-counting*

Counting errors can indicate poor auditory sequential memory. If there are errors in this section, spend plenty of time developing counting skills into the higher decades until automaticity is achieved. When this is achieved the child will be able to count forwards or backwards from any number fluently. Have counters available to use if necessary. To start with encourage children to count onto a number track. Later introduce number lines to help them with calculation.

The difference between a number track and a number line:

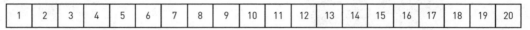

A number track shows whole numbers. Each number occupies a defined space on the track.

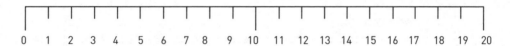

A number line shows whole numbers equidistant on a line. Fractions can also be shown on the number line.

Teach basic counting skills

Practise oral counting as well as counting actual items. The child should set the pace and the teacher should match their speed to the child's speed. If they are unable to accurately count orally, count items with them. If children do know the oral counting sequence practice counting forwards and backwards from different numbers. Also regularly practise step-counting in 10s, 5s and 2s.

Play the game 'Untangling -teen and -ty' (page 141) to reinforce the difference between the endings of the '-teen' numbers and the multiples of 10.

Carefully build up knowledge of the way the number system is constructed from groups of ten, and target areas of specific difficulty such as crossover points. Ask the child to count counters and put them into lines as they count. Remember to leave a gap between each ten items counted out to make the base ten structure explicit. However, do not pause between each decade in oral counting as this will interfere with the development of automaticity. Reinforce the structure of the number system by playing Caterpillar Tracks (page 140) and The Estimating Game (page 139).

Concrete materials

It is essential to use a variety of concrete materials. Some children may enjoy counting small models such as teddies and soldiers. The following apparatuses are particularly successful: base ten material, metre stick, Stern material, Cuisenaire rods and the Slavonic abacus. (See Appendix 8, page 170, for suppliers of equipment.)

Cuisenaire rods, Stern boxes containing blocks, Slavonic abacus, base ten materials.

Cuisenaire rods

Cuisenaire rods are wooden or plastic cuboids coloured according to their length. They are a very useful maths aid. They can be used for learning to count and compare numbers and then to understand calculation. They are a versatile tool which can be used to explore fractions in later numeracy development. Children need to be totally familiar with the Cuisenaire rods and the quantities they represent if they are to use them effectively. Free play is an important part of learning about the relationships between the rods – such as discovering that those of the same length are the same colour, that two rods put end to end will be the same as another rod. The white rod is a 1 cm cube and can be used 'to measure' all the other rods to establish their value.

If the rods are arranged side by side in order of length they form a 'staircase'. Children will often put rods in the wrong places even when they are copying a sequence that has already been modelled. It is important not to point out any error but to help the child to talk about what they doing and discussing the relationships. Suggest they use the white one cube to measure the height of each 'step'. If they do this reasoning and adjusting process for themselves they will start to understand the relationships. An enjoyable game to familiarize children with the rods is The Staircase Game, which is a sequencing game linking the rods to the numbers (see page 142).

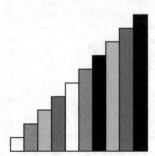

Cuisenaire rod staircase.

Writing numbers

The child should be able to write the dictated numbers reasonably quickly with the digits in the correct sequence and the right orientation. Numbers above 1,000 should be divided appropriately using a space or a comma.

Problems may include the following:

- Lack of automaticity so that the child has to start from the beginning each time in order to know what the next number is. (Example: In order to write the number 4, the child has to count from the beginning so says 1, 2, 3 under their breath before writing 4, then says 1, 2, 3, 4 before writing 5, etc. In order to write 13, the child has to count all the way from one or from 10 before being able to write 13.)
- Reversals (e.g. Ɛ for 3, ∂ for 6, ℮ for 9, 4I for 14).
- Digits in the wrong order in multi-digit numbers (e.g. asked to write 984, writes 489).
- Writing the second digit before the first. The answer is correct but they write the second digit on the paper before writing the first digit (e.g. writes 4 before the 1 in 14). This is a coping strategy. It may indicate that writing the '-teen' numbers is difficult, or has been difficult in the past, and this has become a habit.
- The incorrect number of digits. They may write numbers as they hear them spoken, indicating they do not understand the place-value system (e.g. 147 written as 100407 or 10047).
- Errors with numbers containing zeros (e.g. 1004 instead of 104).
- Zeros in the wrong place (e.g. 140 written as 104).
- Writing HTU above digits as they write the number.
- Unsure where the thousands end and the millions start.

Teaching plan: *building numbers; writing numbers; place value*

If the child is not able to produce a number reasonably quickly from dictation, go back and establish efficient and secure counting skills from the beginning of their first error.

Children who write some of their single digits in reverse or backwards may need help with spatial orientation (Nash-Wortham and Hunt 1997). This may form part of a handwriting programme that includes writing numbers as well as letters (Handwriting Without Tears, see Useful websites, page 169).

Children who write digits in the incorrect order need to practise building numbers. This is dealt with in detail in the section on place value on page 100.

If children are unsure about writing the '-teen' numbers but have developed a coping strategy that gives the correct result, it is probably best to leave well alone. They will usually grow out of this problem as their understanding of numbers improves.

Children who write the incorrect number of digits, or have difficulty understanding the role of zeros in multi-digit numbers, will need considerable place-value work. See the place-value section for teaching suggestions. The use of zero should be introduced as a specific teaching point and should be dealt with very carefully. (See page 102 for how to teach zero.) Introduce it at a time when the child is ready and treat it as a completely separate teaching point. (See place-value teaching suggestions.)

Children should be allowed to write HTU above numbers for as long as they feel it is necessary. This is a coping strategy and will probably disappear as the child gains confidence and understanding. Some children find it helpful to colour code the HTU symbols in different colours and write the digits in the corresponding colours. For example, hundreds could be red, tens could be blue, units could be green.

Confusion about where the thousands end and the millions start is caused by a lack of understanding of place value. Work concretely on place-value grids, emphasizing the repeated groups of hundreds, tens and units. (See place-value teaching suggestions, page 100.)

Reading numbers

The child should be able to read numbers accurately and fluently. They should know where to place 'and' when reading larger numbers (e.g. one hundred **and** fifty-seven thousand nine hundred **and** seventy-two).

Problems include:

* sequencing difficulties (e.g. 207 read as 270)
* left to right confusion (e.g. 476 read as 674)
* -teen/-ty confusion (e.g. 670 read as 617).

Teaching plan: *confusion between '-teen' and '-ty'; reading numbers*

Sequencing difficulties may be evidence of an eye tracking problem. This means that the eye muscles may produce irregular saccades (jumps) as the child reads. This will need investigation by an optometrist (rather than an optician).

Sequencing difficulties might be caused by lack of stable sequencing skills so that the child loses track of which is the next number in the left to right sequence. Left/right confusion can be particularly obvious if the child reads the number backwards. The teacher can help by drawing a star on the left-hand side of the multi-digit number.

-Teen/-ty confusion may be caused by weaknesses in auditory discrimination or from long standing confusions that have not been resolved. Children will need careful training to distinguish between the spoken '-teen' and the '-ty' numbers with the teacher exaggerating the difference. Ensure that the child articulates the names slowly and clearly. Children with a history of speech difficulties often find it difficult to perceive or be aware of the 'n' at the end of the -teen number names. Children who are completely unaware of the 'n' sound at the end of the -teen numbers will need extra training in pronouncing the -teen numbers correctly. Children who can read may benefit from matching the written words with the correct digits. Play 'Untangling -teen and -ty, page 141.

'-teen' numbers
I will be a teenager when I am thir**teen**.

'-ty' numbers
When I am twen**ty** I will drink tea.

Section 2: Calculation

- Knowledge of the key number bonds: bonds of ten, doubles and near doubles.
- Use of basic strategies to calculate efficiently.

Early calculation: addition +1, +2 and subtraction −1, −2

The child should give fluent rapid answers to adding or subtracting one or two. Here the child is not expected to know the answer by rote but to reach the answer from their ability to count one or two forwards or backwards.

Problems include the following.

- Incorrect response (e.g. the child says: 'One more than 12 is 14'. This may show that they are unclear about where to start counting on from. Some children think they should begin with the next number, 13 in this case, then count on 1 to 14).
- Unsure where to start the count when adding 2 (e.g. when they are asked what is 2 more than 12, the child is unsure whether the answer is 13 or 14 because they were not sure whether the count started from 12 or 13).
- Note any 'f/th' confusion caused by poor auditory discrimination or an inability to say the sounds 'th' and 'f'.
- Difficulty with numbers starting with 'thir' (13 or 30) or 'fif' (15 or 50) caused by not relating them to three and five.
- Counts all the numbers from the beginning of the counting sequence (e.g. what is 2 more than 5? The child responds: 1, 2, 3, 4, 5, 6, 7).
- Does not understand what 'more than' means or confuses 'more than' with 'less than'.
- Using their fingers.
- Unable to count backwards.
- Finds counting back two harder than counting back one.

> **Teaching plan: *oral sequences; counting all; counting on; concept of quantity; counting back; confusion between '-teen' and '-ty'***
>
> If the child gives an incorrect response consider the nature of the error. For example, if the child says that one more than 12 is 14 this may because the child does not know the counting sequence. However, it may also be because the child is unsure where to start from when adding one. The teacher will need to spend time revising basic counting skills below 20. See number sense and counting (page 84). Play The Estimating Game (page 139) and Caterpillar Tracks (page 140).
>
> Errors with the numbers 13, 14 and 15 may stem from poor auditory discrimination between 'f' and 'th' sounds. Auditory discrimination problems may also cause difficulties understanding that there is a difference between 13 and 30 and between 15 and 50. In this case the confusion is caused by the end sounds '-teen' and '-ty' when the 'n' sound is not emphasized at the end of the '-teen' words. Sometimes children will confuse 12 and 20 because both words start with 'tw'. Work will need to be done on increasing the child's ability to discriminate between numbers starting with these sounds, and on the '-teen' and '-ty' endings. Build numbers using base 10 materials laid out in lines so that the difference in quantity is explicit. Both the child and the teacher need to speak slowly and clearly, exaggerating the endings as they read the number names so it becomes quite clear which sound is associated with which number.
>
> If children solve plus one and plus two questions by counting all from the beginning, they are not ready to start to learn to calculate. The child will need extra counting practice until they have acquired automaticity so that they count on one or two from any number easily.
>
> If the child does not understand what 'more than' means or confuses it with 'less than' it will be necessary to spend time on direct language work on these concepts. Children need to use concrete materials, such as counters, base ten material or Cuisenaire rods, to

build numbers and explore the physical size of quantities and use comparative language to describe them in relation to each other.

Some children have difficulty understanding the concept of relative size; that is, that one quantity is being compared to a second quantity. This is especially true when discussing 'more than' because the initial quantity becomes part of the second quantity. The ability to compare objects is an underlying skill which young children may not have mastered by the time they are asked to use it mathematically (Grauberg 1998).

Counting on one or two from a number is acceptable; however, beyond this point they should be using knowledge of number bonds. Children who use fingers may need to do so for reassurance, or out of habit. If they have to use fingers very slowly and carefully the teacher needs to return to the teaching plan in the counting section (page 84) until the child is confident counting on and back from any number.

Many children with difficulties find counting back much harder than counting forwards. Children who find counting backwards extremely difficult, in spite of extra practice, can be trained to find the difference between two numbers by counting up, or counting forwards. This method is known as the shopkeeper's method or complementary addition. It is discussed in detail in the place-value section under subtraction (see page 110).

Doubles and near doubles

The doubles facts up to $10 + 10$ should be known 'off by heart'. Children should also be able to explain the relationship between doubles and near doubles, showing they understand that if $2 + 2 = 4$ then $2 + 3$ must equal one more than 4. If they do not understand this it indicates that they have weak reasoning ability about numbers.

The child should be able to apply the doubles facts to higher values through the decades up to 100 and beyond. (Example: If $3 + 3 = 6$, the child should be able to reason that $30 + 30 = 60$. They should also be able to work out that $13 + 3 = 16$ and $53 + 3 = 56$ by applying the same fact. The mantra 'same fact different value' can be useful.)

Note if the child is using a strategy, such as:

- deriving an answer from a known fact, e.g. $5 + 5$ is 10 therefore $6 + 6$ is two more than ten
- using a calculation strategy such as bridging, e.g. $6 + 7 = (6 + 4) + 3 = 10 + 3 = 13$.

(Bridging is discussed fully on page 104.)

Problems may include:

- using fingers to count
- counting all (when adding 3 more on to 4, the child will count 1, 2, 3, 4 … 5, 6, 7)
- counting on in ones from the first number instead of knowing the fact automatically (e.g. $4 + 5$ the child says '4 … 5, 6, 7, 8, 9').

Teaching plan: *building doubles and near doubles, explaining thinking*

Remember that it is essential that the child talks and explains their reasoning. The best way to encourage this is for the child to use concrete materials and talk about what they are doing. Start work on the doubles by using Stern materials or Cuisenaire rods.

2 = 1 + 1
4 = 2 + 2
6 = 3 + 3
8 = 4 + 4
10 = 5 + 5

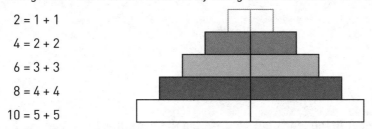

Some children are never able to remember these doubles facts off by heart. These children may need to reason the answers every time, possibly for ever. The best strategy to do this is to bridge through ten. Example: 7 + 7 = (7 + 3) + 4 = 14. (See Bridging Through 10, page 105).

Near doubles

Ideally, children should be able to express in their own words and in their own way that if 2 and 2 is 4 then 2 and 3 must be 5 because it is one more than 4.

1 + 1 = 2
1 + 2 = 3

2 + 2 = 4
2 + 3 = 5

3 + 3 = 6
3 + 4 = 7

4 + 4 = 8
4 + 5 = 9

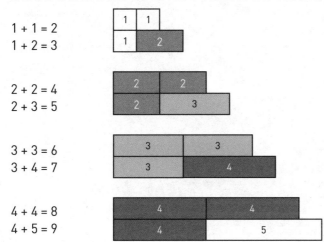

Cuisenaire rods showing the relationships between doubles and near doubles.

Dot patterns

If the child is using fingers for these types of calculations, they should move straight on to studying the dot patterns up to ten as described on pages 95 and 135. These are designed to help the child develop a concept of number. The child should be trained to talk about the patterns and the patterns and their relationships, e.g. shown the dot pattern the child says, 'Seven is made of four and three'.

If the child is counting all, they must be trained not to count every item. One of the most enjoyable ways to do this is to play The Tins Game (see page 148).

Children who count on in ones from the first number mentioned in the question need to be trained to use more accurate strategies; bridging is usually the best strategy to teach in this situation.

93

Triads

Triads are another useful way to record numbers and make the relationship between the number and its components clear. A triad looks like this:

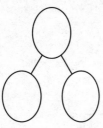

Write the number in the top circle. Now record the two component parts and write these in the lower circles.

Example: Triad showing 5 = 2 + 3
Explain to the child that the triad can be read in different ways.
5 is made of 2 and 3
5 is made of 3 and 2
2 and 3 makes 5
3 and 2 makes 5
5 minus 3 is 2
5 minus 2 is 3

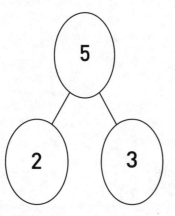

Give the child plenty of practice reading and writing triads. Once the child is familiar with the triad form it provides a clear way to express number relationships. Giving the child a series of partially completed triads and asking them to fill them in is a good way of encouraging a child to talk about numbers.

Later the child could write the sums that the triads represent in the same way as they talked about the dot patterns above.

Start using triads to represent the doubles and near doubles bonds. Later move on to the bonds, or components, of the numbers between 1 and 9.

Dot patterns knowledge

The dot patterns are derived from the conventional dice patterns. For clarity we refer to the patterns for all the numbers from one to ten as the dot patterns. The dot patterns help children develop a sense of what a number is as well as helping them to learn the doubles and near doubles bonds. Accept any reasonably accurate version of the usual dice patterns up to six. Look at the new patterns they have created for the numbers seven to ten. Accept any creative suggestion that combines two of the other dice patterns or a reasonable alternative. However, in due course teach the patterns which emphasize the key facts of the doubles and near doubles.

Problems include:

- poor spatial ability – unable to organize dots in a recognizable form
- randomly scattered dots – may indicate poor visual memory
- putting the counters in single lines – may indicate poor pattern awareness.

Teaching plan: *dot patterns*

If the child does not know the essential facts automatically, these will need to be taught systematically before they can move on. Teach the number bonds by studying the conventional dice patterns up to six, and later dot patterns up to ten. (See instructions for teaching dot patterns on page 135.)

Dot patterns from 1–6.

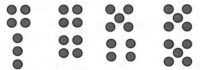

Dot patterns for 7, 8, 9 and 10.

If the child is unable to draw the dots in an easily recognizable form, they may have poor drawing ability or poor spatial awareness. This may be an indication of dyspraxia and they might need to be referred for occupational therapy. It is helpful to give these children small circular stickers so that they can form their patterns by sticking them onto the paper rather than by drawing.

If the child shows no sign of having any recollection of the usual dice patterns (1–6) this indicates a poor visual memory. Train them to build the patterns and to copy the patterns by looking at the patterns on a dice briefly for a few seconds before reproducing them.

If the child demonstrates weak pattern awareness by putting the counters in single lines without a sign of any pattern, the child may need extensive practice to learn the dot patterns.

Numbers 1 to 9

The child should have quick recall of the key number bonds: doubles and near doubles. Some children may be able to learn them off by heart. Children should learn to derive all the other number bonds for the counting numbers from these key facts. Some children will not be able to remember the doubles and near doubles. These children will have to be taught to use a bridging strategy as discussed on page 104.

Key number bonds

Doubles	Near doubles
2 = 1 + 1	3 = 2 + 1
4 = 2 + 2	5 = 3 + 2
6 = 3 + 3	7 = 4 + 3
8 = 4 + 4	9 = 5 + 4
10 = 5 + 5	

Note whether the child is solving missing addend questions by using their known facts or their reasoning. Example: 3 + ? = 7. Do they know that 7 is made of 3 and 4, or do they have to solve it by counting on from 3 to 7 (finding the difference between 3 and 7) to get the answer of 4?

Problems may include:
- using fingers – the child may put 7 fingers up and split the whole number into two smaller numbers, e.g. 7 is made of 3 fingers and 4 fingers
- counting all – counting from 1 to 7 and then working out how many were missing
- counting on from the number given to reach the total
- poor reasoning or poor memory.

Teaching plan: *doubles and near doubles number bonds*

If the child does not know the essential doubles and near doubles number bonds, these will need to be taught systematically before they can move on. Teach these bonds by using concrete materials which give a strong visual image to make the number bonds explicit such as Stern blocks or Cuisenaire rods and studying the dot patterns. (See page 135.)

The dot patterns can help children who have difficulty learning the key number bonds off by heart. By building the dot patterns and talking about them they learn to visualize the numbers and the doubles and near doubles that they are made of. Visualizing means being able to imagine the patterns, even when they are not present, and using this image to calculate (e.g. 7 is made of 3 and 4). From this they learn to reason that 7 take away 3 leaves the 4 and 7 take away 4 leaves 3. Remember that it is essential that the child explains their reasoning route to the teacher. If they are unable to do this, at first the teacher may have to model this strategy themselves. Merely learning to recite a recipe is almost always of limited use at the time and of no use on subsequent occasions. Children must use their own words to reason from first principles if they are to use that reasoning route again.

From each dot pattern, children should be able to reason the following in words. For example, from the pattern of 7 they should be able generate the following:

7 = 3 + 4
7 = 4 + 3
7 – 3 = 4
7 – 4 = 3

Playing games is a good way to teach the dot patterns. Not only do they provide repeated practice but they foster a positive attitude to numeracy as long as the child enjoys them. (See page 143–145.)

Teaching plan: *all number bonds of numbers between 1 and 9; commutativity*

Partitioning

Partitioning numbers means being able to name the constituent parts of a multi-digit number. It is a difficult concept for some children and they find the word itself confusing. It is better for young children to use the simpler form 'is made of'. This also avoids confusion when teaching place-value positions. In primary school, children are taught to partition numbers into hundreds, tens and units. It is less confusing for them to use the word 'partitioning' in this context. The wider meaning of the word can be introduced when they are ready to learn other more flexible ways of partitioning such as seeing 23 as not just 20 + 3 but also as 13 + 10.

The dot patterns introduce the idea of parts, or components, of numbers in an easily accessible way. They emphasize the fact that numbers are made of smaller numbers and provide a strong visual image from which children can reason about number facts and the relationships between them. (For example, the number pattern for 10 shows clearly that 10 is made of two fives.)

Cuisenaire rods

Cuisenaire rods are particularly good tools to use for teaching the number bonds of the single-digit numbers. The child uses the Cuisenaire rods to explore the different combinations of rods that will be the same length as another rod. If the combinations are put out in a structured way they form a clear pattern. An easy way to describe the structure is to call it a 'rod sandwich'. Two rods of the largest number represents the bread with the other pairs of numbers forming the 'filling'. Children can then talk about and reason about the combinations. The commutativity principle is clearly seen: the same two digits make 6 which ever order they are added in.

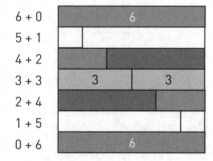

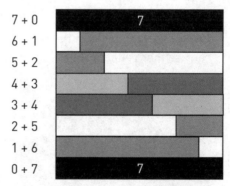

The Cuisenaire 'rod sandwich' for 6 showing all the components of 6.

The Cuisenaire 'rod sandwich' for 7 showing all the components of 7.

Bonds of numbers ten and above to 100

The bonds of ten are the most important number bonds.

Recall of the pairs of numbers that make ten should be automatic. Without this knowledge children are left with very few other strategies for calculating efficiently in the higher decades.

The bonds of ten should be learnt and revised and checked regularly to ensure that they remain firmly lodged in the child's long-term memory. Even if the child cannot recall any other number bonds **they must learn the bonds of ten** if at all possible. These facts underpin calculation throughout the number system. They are the key to understanding place value and are essential if the child is to use the bridging strategy for mental calculation.

Bonds of ten Recall of the pairs of numbers that make ten should be automatic. Without this knowledge children are left with very few other strategies for calculating efficiently in the higher decades.

Teaching plan: *bonds of ten*

Children need to know facts of ten automatically, or be able to derive them quickly, before they can continue on to more complex work. These number facts should be explicitly taught and revised regularly. Teach them by working with concrete materials such as counters, base ten material, Stern material, Cuisenaire rods, a Slavonic abacus and bead strings. (Details of where to obtain these are in Appendix 8, page 170.)

Counters

Put out the dot pattern for ten. Move the counters to show the different pairs of numbers that can make ten.

Cuisenaire rods

These very clearly show the various bonds that make ten. However, the child needs to be thoroughly familiar with the rods and the number that each colour represents before they can use them effectively. (See page 136 for bonds of ten activities.)

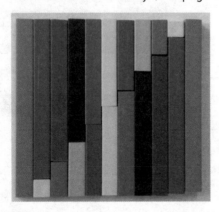

Cuisenaire rods

Slavonic abacus

Bead strings

These are strings of ten beads which can be moved to show pairs of numbers that make ten. They are particularly good for learning subtraction and the concept of the missing addend.

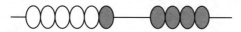

A bead string showing 6 + 4

If a child is unable to remember the bonds of ten, they should be trained to derive the answer by efficient counting on from the larger number. However, this is a last resort. It can take months before children are proficient with number bonds so allow plenty of time and repeated practice. (There are bonds of ten games in Chapter 6.)

Number bonds through the decades

The child should be able to apply their bonds of ten knowledge to numbers in the higher decades. e.g. $84 + 6 = 80 + (4 + 6) = 90$

Problems include:
- needing to use a number line which shows they are not able to apply their bonds of ten knowledge
- counting forwards or backwards in ones
- using their fingers which shows a lack of number bond knowledge or the ability to apply that knowledge.

Teaching plan: *applying bonds of ten to larger numbers*

If children are having problems applying these number bonds through the decades, teach them concretely using rods on place-value grids or in lines. (See the game First to 30, page 150.) Children can be taught to use a bridging strategy on a number line. This strategy is explained on page 104.

Number bonds of 100

The child should be able to apply their bonds of ten knowledge to numbers making 100.
For example:
$90 + ? = 100$ 'Nine and one makes ten therefore 90 and ten will make 100'.
$40 + ? = 100$ 'Four plus six makes ten therefore 40 needs 60 to make 100'.

Problems:
- not realizing that if nine needs one more to make ten, then 90 will need 10 more to make 100
- needing to use a number line which shows they are not able to apply their facts of ten knowledge
- using their fingers, which shows a lack of number bond knowledge or the ability to apply that knowledge.

Teaching plan: *number bonds of multiples of ten*

The best way to teach this is to build the numbers on a 100 square using base ten material or Cuisenaire rods. This reinforces the facts with a strong visual image.

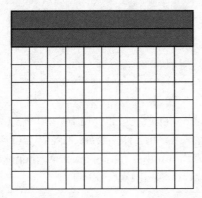

Cuisenaire rods showing 20 on a 100 square.
Therefore you need 80 more to make 100.

Section 3: Place value

The place-value grid

Numbers are made up from individual symbols, called digits, which are combined in very structured ways. The value of a digit in a number depends on its position, or place, in that number.

Numbers are made from the digits 0 to 9 which are combined in structured ways to form all the numbers we use from the smallest fraction to the largest number. It is similar to the way words are made from the letters of the alphabet. For instance, using the four letters o, p, s, t will give post, pots, spot, stop, tops – all with very different meanings depending how the letters are arranged. In a similar way digits are put in a particular order to indicate their value. For example: 6 in these numbers means 600 or 60 or 6:

672   261   856

We call this structure the **place-value grid**. The place-value grid is ordered into columns. Each column varies by a factor of 10; this gives us the names of the column headings. (Although we do not write the names out, the headings are understood to be there.)

The names are **units, tens, hundreds, thousands, tens of thousands, hundreds of thousands, millions**, etc. When we write large numbers, we use commas to make them easier to read. The commas mark off clusters of three: HTU (**hundreds, tens** and **units**). These three names are repeated inside each of the larger groups.

MILLIONS			THOUSANDS			UNITS		
Hundreds	Tens	Units	Hundreds	Tens	Units	Hundreds	Tens	Units
H	T	U	H	T	U	H	T	U

Children without a strong sense of number often fail to grasp the place-value system. They need to use concrete materials, with the teacher giving clear guidance on the significance of the position of the digits in the number. They need to understand that the position or 'place' of the digit in the number changes its value.

Children should be able to partition a number into hundreds, tens and units.

Example: 256 = 2 hundreds, 5 tens and 6 units

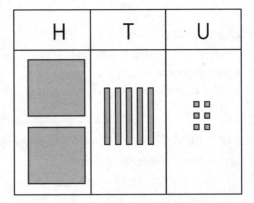

Base ten material showing how 256 consists of 2 hundreds, 5 tens and 6 units.

Teaching plan: *HTU; using the place-value grid; repeating pattern of HTU in large numbers; partitioning into HTU*

In the early stages of teaching place value, use concrete materials on a place-value grid. It may take weeks, or even months, before the child understands the concept. It is best to display all three place-value columns – hundreds, tens and units (HTU) – unless the child is very young. In that case it is reasonable to start with the tens and units columns, especially if the child's peer group is only working at that stage.

It is crucial to introduce the place-value grid gradually and in a structured progressive manner. The place-value grid is a large diagram with three columns headed Hundreds, Tens and Units. There is space for the child to build numbers by putting concrete materials representing the quantities in each column. When the child is comfortable working with HTU introduce three more HTU columns to represent the places within the thousands. Later the repeating pattern of three columns can be extended to the millions and higher numbers.

Hundreds	Tens	Units
100 100 100	‖‖‖	⣿⣿

Base ten material used to build 349 on a place-value grid.

Ten plus a single-digit number

There should be a prompt response to knowing ten plus a single digit produces an answer that is a '-teen' number. The child should be fully aware that the answer to this sort of question is reliable. Note the child who solves this slowly and uncertainly, counting on from the ten to the answer. Other children with strong number sense will solve this type of problem in seconds, often commenting how easy it is.

> e.g. 10 + 4 = 14

Problems may include:
- counting all the way from one
- counting on from ten
- lack of use of the knowledge that 14 is made of one ten and four units.

Teaching plan: *10 plus a single-digit number*

Counting from one

If the child has solved 10 + 4 by counting in ones from 1 this represents a more serious problem. It means that the child has not gained the skill of 'counting on'. Start teaching by developing counting on from any number, before attempting to combine numbers.

Counting on from 10 in ones

If the child counts on from 10 in ones to reach the answer, build numbers on a place-value grid using base ten materials. Teach the child to place one ten in the tens column and add the single-digit number into the units column. It is helpful to place the counters in the dot patterns in the unit column as discussed earlier. Encourage the child to talk about what they are doing and what it means to them. In time they will realize that there is a clear pattern. It should become obvious to the child that if you are adding 4 to ten the answer will start with the word four as in fourteen.

Calculations with the -teen numbers are usually very problematic for children with low numeracy. The question mentions ten first and then four next but the answer is the reverse: four is mentioned first as in fourteen. Those who find this difficult will need these types of questions and answers to be modelled and demonstrated by the teacher many times.

Children who cannot express the -teen numbers quickly and easily should return to practising counting the numbers 10 to 20 until counting, building and naming the -teen numbers is fully automatized and produced effortlessly.

If the child does not understand that 14 is made of one ten and four units, once again building the -teens numbers on the grid will be a teaching priority.

The value of zero

Many children are confused about the value of zero. When they first encounter zero they have sometimes been told it means 'nothing'. This idea may persist and they think that zero means nothing so it can be omitted or ignored.

The best way to teach 'zero' is to explore the idea concretely on a place-value grid showing how 10 is made of one ten and no units. The child needs to understand the principle of exchange; the rule is that the moment you have 10 ones in the units column they must be exchanged for one tens rod. (If the child is uncertain about this, play some exchange games; see page 149.)

Ask the child to put out the dot pattern for 9 on the place-value grid. Add 1 to make 10. Now exchange the ten ones for one ten. Make sure that the child lines the ones up next to the tens when they do they exchange. The one ten is placed in the tens column. Ask the child what they can see in the units column. They need to answer in a sentence such as 'The units column is empty', 'There is nothing in the units column' or 'There are no ones in the units column'. Ask the child to place a card with 0 written on it to remind you that there are no ones in the units column. The advantage of showing it this way is that there is a strong visual image of one ten rod and a 0 which is visually similar to the written number 10.

Many children see 10 as a unitary amount that comes after 9. Considerable time needs to be spent with some children to explain that 10 is recorded as a one and a zero to show one ten and no units. (This work is best done after children are familiar with building -teen numbers, such as 14 being made of one ten and four units.)

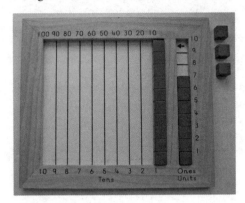

Stern dual board.

Another very useful piece of equipment is the Stern dual board. This shows how ten unit blocks can be exchanged for one ten block. The number can then be read off the lower part as 1 ten and 0 units: 10.

This process can be repeated to show how larger multiples of 10 are built.

To fully understand the importance of zero as a place holder, children need to practise writing numbers up to 1,000,000 on a place-value grid and to talk about the value of the one in numbers above 10, as in one hundred, one thousand, ten thousand, one hundred thousand, one million and so on.

Billions			Millions			Thousands			Units		
H	T	U	H	T	U	H	T	U	H	T	U
									1	0	0
								1	0	0	0
							1	0	0	0	0
						1	0	0	0	0	0
					1	0	0	0	0	0	0

Billions			Millions			Thousands			Units		
H	T	U	H	T	U	H	T	U	H	T	U
		1	8	0 ,	4	5	9 ,	0	6	2	

One hundred and eighty million, four hundred and fifty-nine thousand, and sixty-two.

Bridging

Bridging through ten is a strategy that makes it easier to add a single digit to a number to make a quantity bigger than ten. Bridging 'through ten' involves using 10 as a 'stepping stone' in calculation. (Later it can be applied to multiples of ten.) Children need to know the bonds of ten and all the number bonds of the numbers 2 to 9 in order to use the strategy.

The child should be able to use the bridging strategy to add a single digit to a number.

The child also needs to understand the principle of exchange before they can apply the bridging strategy. The child needs to know that 10 ones can be exchanged for one 10.

Example: 8 + 5

In order to bridge through 10 the child needs to know that 8 and 2 makes 10. Then 5 can be partitioned into 2 and 3. The sum can now be written as 8 + 2 + 3 = 10 + 3 = 13. This can be clearly shown using concrete materials or a number line.

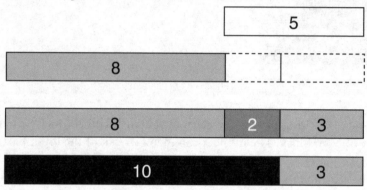

Bridging using Cuisenaire rods.

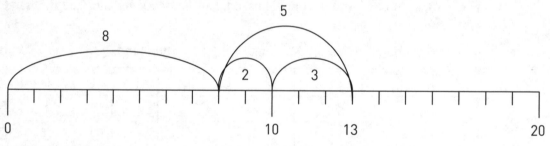

Bridging on a number line.

Problems may include
- counting in ones, showing no place-value knowledge
- counting on in ones from the first number mentioned
- confused place-value knowledge: adding tens digit to the unit digit, e.g. 23 + 4 and give the answer 53 because they have added the units to the tens.

Teaching plan: *bridging through 10; principle of exchange*

The child should be able to use the bridging strategy to add two numbers that total more than ten.

Counting in ones

If children are counting on in ones when adding single digits to each other teach the bridging strategy. This is best demonstrated using counters on a structured number track that clearly shows the end of each group of ten. (See the game Caterpillar Tracks, page 140.)

Train the child to complete the first ten and see what is left to be placed on the next ten's track. In this way they build up a strong image that can be visualized when the track is not present.

Example: 8 + 5

8 + 5 = 10 + 3

10 + 3 = 13

Number track showing how the tens structure is made explicit.

The Stern dual board (see www.mathsextra.com) is very useful for teaching bridging because it shows concretely that it is easier and quicker not to count on in ones. Children see that it is easier to split the second digit into the number bond required to make 10 and then add on the units that are left.

Example: 8 + 5

8 + 5 can be regrouped as (8 + 2) + 3 = 10 + 3 = 13

The dual board is also ideal for teaching bridging on harder examples through the higher decades where the answer is less than 100.

Example: 24 + 7

Can be regrouped as (24 + 6) + 1. This is very clear when built and rearranged using bridging concretely on the dual board.

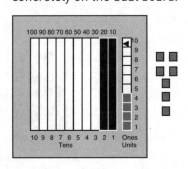

24 + 7 = 2 tens and 4 units plus 7 units

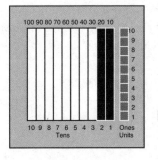

2 tens , 10 units and 1 unit

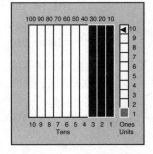

3 tens and 1 unit

Stern dual board.

How to use the place-value grid
Example: 37 add 5
Build 37 on the grid using base ten materials.

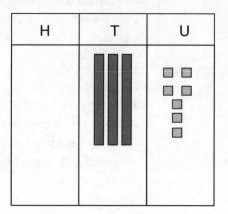

3 tens and 7 units

Next build 5 underneath the 7 on the grid.

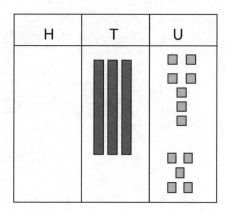

3 tens and 7 units plus 5 units

Discuss the fact that addition requires combining the top number on the grid with the bottom number on the grid. By moving the unit counters and discussing what they are doing the child may discover that there are more than 10 in the units column.

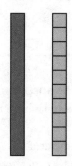

Exchanging 10 ones for 1 ten.

They should know that 10 ones can be exchanged for one 10 which is then placed in the tens column. The answer is read off the grid by looking at how many tens and how many units there are on the grid.

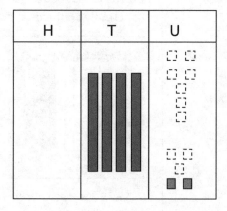

4 tens and 2 units = 42

Teaching the principle of exchange

If the child has difficulties, or does not know about exchanging the ten ones for one ten, teach the principle of exchange: that several items can be exchanged for one of greater value. Some children may respond well to questions about possible solutions to the problem of having too many ones in the units column and may come up with a solution for themselves through dialogue. If the child works it out by talking and reasoning, they are likely to develop a better understanding than being shown directly. However, if the child cannot do this, teach the principle of exchange through practical games and activities. (See First to 30, Back Track, pages 150–51.)

Confused place-value knowledge

A child who is confused about place-value knowledge may add a tens digit to a units digit. Return to building multi-digit numbers on the place-value grid, practising putting either more tens or more units in the correct position until the process is performed by the child without undue effort. Gradually, the child will show when they are ready to relinquish the concrete apparatus.

Unit subtraction

Children should be able to answer promptly when they subtract a single digit from a two-digit number where there are the same quantity of units in both numbers.

For example, understanding that $36 - 6$ must be 30. They should demonstrate or explain that 36 is made from 30 and 6 or can be expressed as 3 tens and 6 units. Therefore if 6 units are removed, then 30, or 3 tens, remain. Some children will know this so instinctively that they may not be able to explain why it is easy for them. These children have an intuitive sense of number. Others who show little or none of this intuition will need considerable guided help to come to understand the process.

Problems may include:

- counting back in ones
- confused place-value knowledge, e.g. $36 - 6$ the answer is given as 3 because they have correctly subtracted the 6 but do not understand that a zero is necessary to express 30
- taking the single digit from the tens number, e.g. $53 - 3 = 2$. The response is 2 because they have subtracted 3 from the tens instead of from the units.
- lack of understanding that 36 is made of three tens and six units.

> ### Teaching plan: *subtracting the same digit; revise place value*
>
> #### Unit subtraction
>
> Children should be able to subtract a single digit from a number easily when the unit amounts are the same. If they are not able to do so, they need to develop their understanding of place value. Work on building numbers on the place-value grid or use the Stern dual board. Focus on subtracting the same quantity of units as in the larger number as in 36 – 6 or 24 – 4. Continue to revise this work until the child can solve this kind of problem without hesitation.
>
> If the child shows place-value confusion by subtracting the single-digit number from the tens number as in 32 – 2 = 12 then continue building numbers of increasing complexity on the place-value grid or with the Stern dual board.
>
> The error 76 – 6 = 7 is caused by the child not understanding that the value of the digit depends on its position in the number. Revise place-value work as described earlier, before attempting further calculations.
>
> Children can use base 10 material to build numbers in horizontal lines.
>
> **Example:** the number 36 in a horizontal line consists of 3 tens and 6 ones. It is clear that subtracting 6 by removing the 6 ones leaves the answer 30 clearly visible.
>
> Base ten material showing that 36 – 6 = 30
> 36 laid out in base ten material;
> after 6 are taken away there are 30 left.

Adding and subtracting 1s, 10s, 100s, 1000s

Children should use their place-value knowledge to calculate instinctively and produce a prompt answer.

Addition skills should be flexible, adding the smaller number to the appropriate digit in the larger number as appropriate.

Children should be able to solve simple calculations mentally, but look for evidence of their ability to record their thinking in some way on paper, either as they are working or when you ask them to explain or show you how they solved the problems.

Example: 20 + 10 = 30 (perhaps explaining to you '2 tens plus one more ten makes 3 tens or 30')

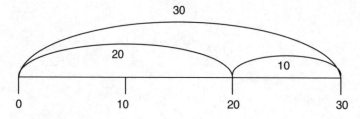

Number line showing 20 + 10.

Problems or strategies to note:
- needing to write HTU as a guide or reminder above the numbers before calculating
- counting on or counting back in ones rather than tens or hundreds
- counting backwards from the larger number, e.g. in 20 – 10
- use of fingers
- addition in columns; this indicates they are applying a 'recipe' because they do not understand place value.

Teaching plan: *calculating with 10, 100, 1000*

Adding and subtracting 1s, 10s, 100s, 1000s

Children should use their place-value knowledge to calculate swiftly.

If children are not using their place-value knowledge to calculate in this section automatically, teach each item very systematically. At first, practise adding and subtracting ones to various numbers, gradually increasing the size of the numbers as the child's confidence increases.

If these addition skills are inflexible so the child is unable apply them in different situations, they should work on the place-value grid. Practise building numbers. Start with the largest number, then add the smaller number to it. Place the appropriate quantities in the correct positions on the place-value grid. If a child still needs to write HTU above numbers before calculating allow them to do so; the need will go away naturally, when the child feels confident.

If the child is counting on, or counting back, in ones teach them to build numbers with base ten materials.

Work until the child is able to immediately solve the problem concretely. In time the aim is that they will be able to visualize the concrete materials, even when they are not present.

Example: 256 – 100 on the place-value grid

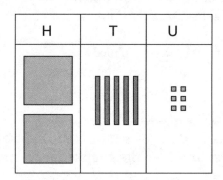 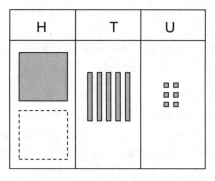

Build 256   Take away 100

If children remain confused, go back to more basic work building numbers and breaking numbers down on the place-value grid. (See place-value games beginning on page 149.) Children could also be trained to demonstrate this procedure on a number line using as few jumps as possible: in this case, only a single jump.

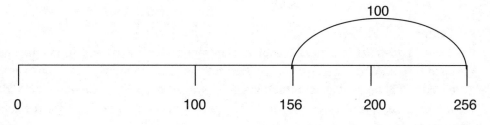

Number line showing 256 – 100

If children are still using their fingers, analyse carefully what they are using their fingers for. Some children with severe memory problems may be using their fingers very sensibly to record how many tens they have subtracted, or how many hundreds they have subtracted. This sort of use should not be discouraged. The habit will gradually diminish as the child's confidence increases.

However, if the child is using fingers for counting in ones this should be discouraged. Consolidation work will need to be carried out at a much more basic level. Return to an earlier level of teaching. Learning the dot patterns will help children to stop using fingers and counting in ones. (See dot pattern activities, page 135.)

It is important to train them to use chunking methods instead of ones. Chunking involves grouping a small number of items together so that five ones would be thought of as a 'chunk' of 5.

Subtraction

A prompt response is required to display their use of place-value knowledge. These items assess the ability to use automatic intuitive knowledge and their ability to apply efficient strategies:

- recognizing number combinations as part of doubles patterns: $10 - 5 = 5$ (because $5 + 5 = 10$)
- bridging back through ten, e.g. $15 - 6 = (15 - 5) - 1 = 10 - 1 = 9$
- complementary addition (working forwards via tens or using a number line).

Problems or strategies to note:
- counting back in ones
- bridging back through ten where applying doubles knowledge would be more appropriate, e.g. $14 - 7 = (14 - 4) - 3 = 7$ (this is evidence of mathematical reasoning but is less efficient and slower than noticing the doubles pattern, e.g. $14 - 7 = 7$; the slower strategy requires more working memory)
- the use of number lines is a good strategy if it is correctly applied
- subtraction in columns (if they can only do it this way, observe exactly how they do the procedure).

> ### Teaching plan: *subtracting strategies – doubles subtraction; subtracting back (bridging back); complementary addition (the shopkeeper's method)*
>
> If a child is counting back in ones they are not ready to learn subtraction strategies. They will need more practice at counting and working with number bonds.
>
> Teach the child the subtraction strategies: recognizing doubles patterns, bridging back, and complementary addition. However, not all children are able to use these strategies as is discussed below. If a child is using a different but effective strategy consistently, allow them to continue to do so. An effective strategy is one that can be applied to similar mathematical problems.
>
> #### Doubles subtraction
>
> If a child does not recognize a doubles subtraction such as $14 - 7$, revise the doubles facts up to $10 + 10$. When they are secure at using this strategy, provide revision examples, some of which will be doubles subtractions but some will not. Encourage the child to talk about why one example uses a doubles strategy and another does not. Explore the concept using Cuisenaire rods and triads.
>
> #### Concrete and written forms of demonstrating 14 – 7
>
> Write or make the number 14 then show the double that it can be made of.
>
> Encourage the child to use language to reason that 14 is made of 7 and 7 so if one 7 is removed then the other 7 remains. This can be shown concretely with Cuisenaire rods, showing that 14 is built from a ten and a four rod, which is equivalent to two seven rods. It can be written as a triad which clearly shows the relationship between 14 and 7 and 7.

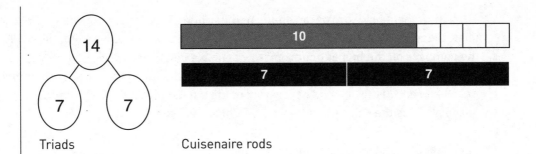

Triads   Cuisenaire rods

Subtracting back (bridging back)

Children should be able to use a bridging strategy to subtract back. Mastering the technique will be useful for the future when they are working on higher numbers. However, many children with low numeracy find working backwards very difficult indeed and are unable to use this strategy despite careful teaching. In that case teach complementary addition which works forwards instead. Complementary addition is discussed below.

Bridging back is a useful strategy when the number being subtracted is a one-digit number. Teach children to visualize counting back by applying their number-bonds knowledge through the ten or tens number. Example: 15 – 6 = (15 – 5) – 1 because 6 is made of 5 and 1. Thus 15 – 6 = (15 – 5) – 1 = 10 – 1 = 9.

Children who cannot imagine this should be taught to record their thinking on a number line showing their first jump back to the tens number and their second jump back to complete the process. This approach is useful even if the child is poor at placing numbers at appropriate places on the number line. (Do revision work on the relative positions of numbers on a number line as an estimating activity.)

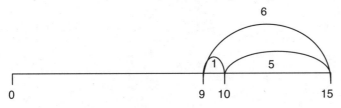

Number line showing 15 – 6 by bridging back through 10.

Complementary addition (the shopkeeper's method)

This is also known as the shopkeeper's method because, before the use of tills, this was the usual method for giving change in everyday shopping situations.

If children have been counting back in ones, or find bridging back difficult, show them how complementary addition works. Demonstrate that a line of items contains the same number of items no matter which end you start counting. Put a few counters, less than ten, in a line. Ask the child to count them twice, first from one end, then from the other. The child needs to understand that the number remains the same whichever end you start counting from.

Next, show them that the number of counters remaining is always the same, whether you subtract some items from the beginning of the line or the end of the line. Ask the child to show you a few examples, making sure that they talk about it as they do it so that they really believe it.

2 counters removed from the right

2 counters removed from the left

Then show them how to draw an empty number line. (If they have not worked with number lines, these will need to be taught.) Give them plenty of practice at estimating and placing the numbers on the line at approximately sensible distances. Teach children to put a zero to mark the beginning of the number line on the left, then to place the larger number at the right-hand end of the line and next to record the smaller number on the line at an appropriate point. Thus the child will be working from left to right.

Example: 54 – 7 on a number line

0   7   54

Child has marked 7 and 54 at appropriate places on an empty number line.

Remind them of the concrete work that showed the removal of a certain number of items can take place from either end. Then explain that the subtraction of 7 can be represented on the number line by deleting the distance between zero and 7, thereby removing 7. A very powerful way of making the point that 7 is actually removed is to allow the child to use scissors to cut off the distance of 0 to 7.

Number line showing how 7 is removed and the distance remaining is calculated by bridging through 10 and 50.

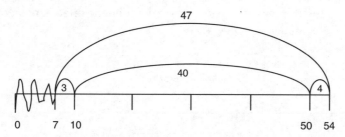

The next step involves finding the 'gap' between 7 and 54 working from left to right. Bridging must be used next so that the child will make one jump from 7 to 10. They should be trained to place the number of steps that one jump represents above the jump curve. From 10 the child jumps to 50, if they can understand this. The child should say what quantity that distance represents. It is 40 in this instance. Finally, the final jump from 50 to 54 is 4 and that is recorded above the curve. The answer is obtained by adding the three numbers above the curve (3 + 40 + 4). If children have any difficulty mentally adding these three numbers in a line or 'string', they will need further addition practice.

   If the child has a tendency to solve these kinds of problems by using many jumps on a number line, gradually help them to use fewer jumps. Instead of jumping four times to represent the distance between 10 and 50, talk with them about the fact that this could be done using one jump of 40 instead. (Some children have difficulty understanding that a number line represents a distance rather than discrete points. In this case they will need to work on measurement and what it means.)

Subtraction in columns
Children should not be using column arithmetic as their preferred method for solving these types of problems.

   They will only develop understanding using formal column arithmetic if they have derived it from working with concrete materials and are able to reason about what they are doing.

Section 4: Multiplication and division

Teach children how to derive multiplication facts and division facts from the key tables facts: 10×
and 5× a number.

Work on multiplication and division together from an early stage in teaching the topic as both
operations involve the concept of groups of objects. Multiplication is based on the total quantity
of items in a specified number of groups. Division, the inverse of multiplication, is based on the
number of groups being discussed. For example, if $4 \times 5 = 20$ then $20 \div 5 = 4$ and $20 \div 4 = 5$. If
four fives are twenty there are four fives in twenty and five fours in twenty.

Although this seems straightforward, many children with low numeracy levels will need to spend
considerable time exploring the links between these two operations which are often artificially
presented separately in many classrooms.

It is important not to use the words 'times', or 'multiply', at this early stage. Many children do
not remember the meaning of 'times', or 'multiply' and the words provoke anxiety. It will be less
threatening to use the transparent form 'four tens' to describe 4 groups of 10. At first only use the
form $10 \times n$ where n is the table being studied, e.g. 10 fours means 10×4 whereas 4 tens means 4×10. It is important to keep to this structure at the early stage. Later the child will learn that changing
the order of multiplication does not change the answer; this follows the commutativity principle.

10 fours

4 tens

Multiplication

The child should know the multiplication facts, or be able to apply reasoning to derive them from
other known facts.

Children should know the key facts: $1 \times n, 5 \times n, 10 \times n$ (n stands for any particular table).

Note whether the children can use the commutativity principle (i.e. 3×4 is the same as 4×3)
correctly or if it is confusing them. It is advisable at first to establish in the child's mind that they
are working on a specific table. Do not make the point too soon that 3×4 is the same as 4×3 as
this usually confuses those with weak numeracy or little understanding. Teach the commutativity
principle later, when they have developed basic understanding, by introducing arrays and the area
model of multiplication (Yeo 2003).

Be aware of the language of multiplication. Does the child understand the use of the word 'times',
as in '5 times 2'? If they do not, omit it and use the clearer more explicit form of '5 twos'.

Some strategies are:

- Reasoning from a known fact by halving, e.g. 5×3. Child knows that 5 is half of 10. They know
  that $10 \times 3 = 30$ and therefore understand 5×3 must be half of 30 which is 15.
- Reasoning from a known fact, e.g. 'I know that five twos are ten, so six twos must be two more
  than ten, which is twelve.'
- Repeated addition of groups, e.g. $3 \times 6 = 6 + 6 + 6$ or 3 groups of 6.

Problems include the following.

- Confused about which table they are working in. Example: If $5 \times 3 = 15$ then unsure whether
  the next fact, 6×3, would be 5 more or 3 more.
- Lack understanding of commutativity. Example: What is 6×2? If the child says: 'I don't know
  my 6 times table' this indicates that they do not understand that they are being asked about the
  2 times table as well. (Do not teach the commutativity principle until the child has developed
  some understanding of multiplication.)
- Only able to step-count starting from the beginning of the sequence. Example: To work out 8×7 they say 7, 14, 21 … to reach 56, rather than step-counting from 35 which is 5×7.

- Being unable to halve numbers easily, especially 30, 50, 70 and 90 (rather than the easier 20, 40, 60 and 80).

The concept of multiplication: counter demonstration The child should be able to put out groups of counters to illustrate a multiplication statement and explain what they have done. For example, 2 threes will be two groups with three in each group.

If the child was able to do this effectively, move on to the tables section. If the child was not able to form appropriate groups, they need to work on the concept before starting to learn tables.

Teaching plan: *concept of multiplication – repeated groups, arrays*

If the child cannot put out groups of counters correctly to illustrate what 2 threes are they need to work on describing exactly what they see in front of them. Looking at counters arranged as shown, they need to say: 'I can see two threes'. (Note: If a child says: I can see 2 threes but I can also see 3 twos, use this as an opportunity to explore the commutativity principle.)

2 threes

During this activity the teacher should model the language used. (Remember to omit the word 'times'. Saying '2 threes' is a more natural form of speech than saying two times three or two groups of three.) Allow the child plenty of practice at describing what they actually see in front of them. When they are consistently correct, show them two threes as well as three twos.

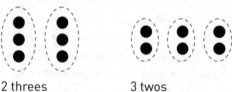

2 threes   3 twos

Ensure the child talks about the difference between the two groups. Practise more examples using different patterns. Ensure that the counters are laid down using the correct dot patterns that explicitly show the difference between 4 threes and 3 fours.

4 threes   3 fours

Children with good spatial abilities may be able to move quickly on to building and laying out arrays, making rectangles with counters.

Example: 3 × 4

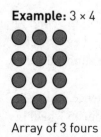

Array of 3 fours

They may realize that they can see 3 fours but also 4 threes in the rectangular array depending on their viewpoint. Those who find this very difficult will not be ready to study this in the array form. This should be revisited at a later point.

Children who know their tables by rote but who cannot demonstrate full understanding using any concrete materials will learn to think more flexibly by using a variety of materials to explore tables in a different way. Remember, it is essential that they talk about what they are doing.

Later on, encourage them to use Cuisenaire rods rather than counters. To demonstrate 3 fours they would select and lay out 3 rods which measure 4 cm each. They can then create a second line showing that 4 threes are the same length as 3 fours.

4 threes

3 fours

Multiplication strategies

Teach 'big-value' strategies for learning tables. Big-value strategies are strategies that can be universally applied to a body of work such as learning all the tables. The big-value strategy for tables is to learn $10 \times n$ and $5 \times n$. All the other tables can be quickly derived from these two (Yeo 2003). Conventional methods of learning tables rely on good verbal memory. However, some children do not remember verbal associations so they keep 'forgetting' their tables.

If children can apply some reasoning to work out unknown tables facts, carefully analyse whether they are using any strategy consistently and correctly. If they are using an efficient enough reasoning strategy, allow them to continue to do so. If they have no strategies or their strategies are too slow to be useful, teach the times tables strategy. This method is ideal for children with very poor rote memories because even when they forget the facts they can reason their way to the answer using this big-value strategy. Some may manage to retain rote knowledge of tables for a while, but many with poor long-term memories will forget facts learnt off by heart over time.

Teach the key table $n \times 10$. Once pupils know the 10 times table teach them to derive the 5 times table from it by reasoning that 5 is half of 10 therefore $n \times 5$ is half of $n \times 10$. Next use arrays of counters, or Cuisenaire rods, to demonstrate that the answer to $n \times 10$ is the same as the answer to $10 \times n$. Once they understand this they are ready to learn more tables. The key facts for each table are $10 \times n$ and $5 \times n$. (See Times table strategy page 116) A suggested order is the 2 times table, the 4 times table, and the 3 times tables followed by the 6 times table, the 8 times table, the 9 times table and the 7 times table.

Times tables strategy

Work on one table at a time.

1. Build children's **feel for multiplication and division** and their understanding of the concepts of multiplication and division.
   — Practise step-counting.
   — Extend children's step-counting skills so they become used to thinking in 'steps' or groups.
   — Build multiplication and division relationships as repeated groups using concrete materials to create strong visual images.
   — Ensure the child talks about what they are doing and the relationships between the numbers.
   — Work on multiplication and division word problems.

2. Build children's **knowledge of the times tables sequences**. Teach children to use a simple universal tables strategy.
   — Learn the key fact $10 \times n$ and revise repeatedly.
   — Derive $5 \times n$ by reasoning from $10 \times n$ [5 is half of 10 therefore $5 \times n$ will be half of $10 \times n$].
   — Learn the key fact $5 \times n$ and revise repeatedly.
   — Reason from key tables facts to figure out other tables facts.
   — Practise using the key facts frequently. With practice children reason increasingly efficiently, and more and more tables are known 'by heart'.

Example for the ×3 table

Key facts: $1 \times 3 = 3$ $5 \times 3 = 15$ $10 \times 3 = 30$

   Other tables facts are derived by reasoning or step-counting from the key facts.

   To work out 7×3 the child reasons: $5 \times 3 = 15$. Seven is two more than 5 so I need to add two more groups of three which is six. So 7×3 will be $15 + 6$ which is 21 [$7 \times 3 = (5 \times 3) + 3 + 3$ or use step-counting 15, 18, 21].

   To work out 9×3 the child reasons from 10×3. The child says: $10 \times 3 = 30$. 9×3 is one less three. Therefore 9×3 is $30 - 3 = 27$.

Summary
- The key tables facts $10 \times n$, $5 \times n$ must be known 'by heart'.
- Children have to practise figuring out other facts using efficient reasoning routes.

Teaching plan: *tables strategies; key facts 10 × n and 5 × n; reasoning to derive other tables; revise step-counting forwards and backwards; practise explaining*

Teaching ×10 and ×5

Counters

Start by asking the child to build the times 10 table facts using counters. Ensure that they talk about what they doing and what it represents. (Example: 5 tens are 50. 4 tens are one less ten than 50, so 4 tens are 40.) Although this takes time, it is essential for the child to build the numbers so they can appreciate their relative size and see the effect of multiplication as repeated addition. (Later children will learn that multiplication can also be shown as an array or the area model.) Pattern cards can be used for speed and convenience as long as the child understands that the dots represent the physical quantities.

Tens rods

Next ask the child to demonstrate 5 tens and 10 tens, placing tens rods horizontally to give a clear image that 5 tens are half of 10 tens.

Revision

Practise the times 5 and times 10 table in random order with oral and written questions. When the child knows the times 5 and times 10 tables start work on the other tables.

Other tables

It is probably best to teach the times 2 table next. After that there is no fixed best order. The ×3 and ×4 tables are usually taught next. However, some children may prefer to tackle one of the 'harder' tables like ×9. If they can manage it they will gain confidence from mastering a difficult tables sequence (Yeo 2003).

Start with the key facts for each table and ask the child to derive the others by reasoning forwards or backwards from the key facts. They should put out counters to demonstrate the table on a table grid as shown below. (Alternatively they could put the counters into small bowls showing two in each bowl.)

Children need to step-count forwards and backwards from the key facts to acquire efficient skills from this strategy. If they are unable to step-count efficiently through a particular table (for example 4, 8, 12, ...), this needs to be practised. However, step-counting using more than two or three steps to reach an answer should be discouraged as it places too much load on the working memory and is too slow to be efficient.

Example: ×2 table on a table grid

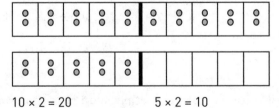

10 twos are twenty.

5 is half of ten so 5 twos are half of 20.
5 twos are 10.

10 × 2 = 20   5 × 2 = 10

If children are confused about which table they are working in, they need to be trained to say which table they are thinking about. Use counters to demonstrate the table being studied by putting out dot patterns. When the child talks about the table they should stress the number of the table they are working on. For example, they would say: '8 **twos** are two less than 10 **twos**. 10 **twos** are 20 so 8 **twos** will be 20 – 2 – 2 which is 16'.

Work forwards from the key facts of 1 two and 5 twos. Practise until the child is able to work easily with one or two steps forwards. For example, 1 × 2 = 2, so 2 twos will be 2 + 2 which is 4. 3 twos will be two more than 2 × 2. So 3 twos will be 2 + 2 + 2 which is 6. Derive 6 twos and 7 twos from 5 × 2 = 10.

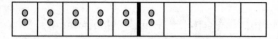

6 × 2

6 **twos** are one more two than 5 **twos**.

5 **twos** are 10 so 6 **twos** will be 10 + 2 which is 12.

Next, practise working backwards from the 5 × 2 = 10 to work out what 4 twos are.
   Then start from 10 × 2 to work out what 9 × 2 and 8 × 2 would be.

8 × 2

8 **twos** are two less than 10 **twos**.

10 **twos** are 20 so 8 **twos** will be 20 – 2 – 2 which is 16. (They should step-count saying 20, 18, 16.)

Arrays and the area model

Use counters to explore setting out multiplication in arrays. This introduces children to the commutativity principle – the fact that the answer to a multiplication sum is the same in whichever order the numbers are multiplied (e.g. 3 × 4 = 12 and 4 × 3 = 12).

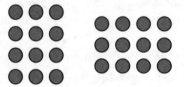

Arrays of 3 fours and 4 threes.

Counters set out in an array form a rectangle which clearly shows the link between multiplication and division. Make sure the child talks about what they are doing and seeing.

   The next step is to teach the child that if the counters are replaced by square units they can work out the area of the rectangle. Use centimetre cubes and 1 cm² paper to make the link between arrays and the area model. Put out the cubes in an array then transfer them to the paper. Colour in the squares on the paper to show the area. Practice putting cubes over the drawing to reinforce the visual image.

   Once they understand the concept, a quick sketch of a rectangle will be sufficient for working out multiplication and division.

Division

Children should be able to derive division facts from multiplication facts and explain what they are doing. For example, they should understand that if 5 × 3 = 15 there must be 5 threes in 15 and 3 fives in 15.

There are two concepts in division: grouping and sharing.

Division involves splitting a quantity into equal parts or groups. This is the grouping model. The grouping concept links directly to the multiplication facts. Example: If 4 × 5 = 20, then 20 ÷ 5 = 4. In the sharing concept of division items are shared equally amongst a known number of groups to find out how many there will be in each group. In both cases the quantity in each group must be the same. If an amount is left over it is called a remainder.

Problems:

- use of fingers
- counting in ones
- drawing tally marks and circling groups to derive the answer
- confusion between the grouping and sharing concepts
- relying on counters or other concrete material.

Teaching plan: *concept of groups; division facts*

Concept of groups

The child should model division with concrete materials and use appropriate language to describe what they have built.

Example: I have built two groups of three.

Now I have built three groups of two.

This can lead on to the language of division:

I have divided 6 into two groups with three items in each group.

I have divided 6 into three groups with two items in each group.

Concept of sharing

The child should explore division by sharing with concrete materials and use appropriate language to describe what they have done. They share out the counters one by one to find out the size of the groups.

Example: 12 ÷ 3

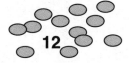

I have a pile of 12 counters and I am going to put them into 3 bowls, so that each bowl has the same number of counters in it.

I have put 12 counters into 3 bowls. Each bowl has 4 counters in it.

Deriving division facts from multiplication facts

If the child cannot derive division facts from multiplication facts, work concretely on laying out repeated groups and asking questions to guide their thinking. The child should answer in full sentences. If the child is anxious, do not use the words 'divide' or 'division' at all as even hearing these words mentioned may increase their anxiety.

Example: 20 ÷ 5

Put counters in groups of five.

Suggested questions for the teacher to ask to guide thinking:

How many fives does it take to build 20? How many groups of 5 are needed to build 20?

Children use their own words to explain that it takes 4 fives to build 20 so there are 4 groups of five in 20.

When the child is confident and successful at answering these kinds of questions, practise writing the multiplication facts in the form 20 = 4 × 5.

Slowly introduce the spoken word 'division'. When the child is comfortable using the word 'division' introduce the division sign. Practise it by getting the child to hear the word, repeat the word, write the division sign and read the division sign using the word 'divide': 20 ÷ 5 = 4. Twenty divided by 5 is four. Do not use the form 5 into 20 at this stage as it causes confusion.

If the child is confused about one item versus one group, spend considerable time building groups of numbers and talking about them using the language of division. For many children it seems confusing to mention the word 'one' when they can see many objects in a group so that when they say 'I can see one group of four' they will often hesitate and lack confidence in their answer. Carry on using this kind of language until children are comfortable and confident.

If children want to draw tally marks and circle groups to derive their answers, encourage them to work with groups containing small numbers of items until they feel very confident. If they try to do this when working with larger groups, spend more time working on the concept rather than drawing huge quantities of tally marks.

If the child uses their fingers to work on division, this should be discouraged as it almost always leads to confusion.

Allow the child to use concrete materials as long as necessary.

Section 5: Word problems

The child should be able to select an appropriate operation and apply it correctly to solve the problem. Teach the child to approach the problem using concrete objects or diagrams to interpret the problem and talk about it.

Problems:

- failing to understand the question
- selecting the wrong operation
- misapplying the operation
- confusion between the division concepts of grouping and sharing.

Teaching plan: *simplify word problems; use items and diagrams to understand word problems; types of word problems*

Teach children to understand the concepts underlying word problems. Beware of training children to look for trigger words which do not always lead to applying the same operation. For instance the word 'altogether' may be used in problems which required different operations.

The **addition** problem: Jon has 5 sweets. His sister has 3 sweets. *How many sweets do they have altogether?*

The **multiplication** problem: There are 4 ponds. There are 2 ducks on each pond. *How many ducks are there altogether?*

Encourage children to use concrete materials to clarify what the question is about. (For young children or those who are very confused use the actual objects, such as sweets, rather than counters.) Then they can draw pictures or diagrams to illustrate their thinking. After that they should write it down in a 'number sentence'. Remember to make sure that children talk about what they are doing and drawing. This multi-sensory approach supports their thinking as well as developing good problem-solving habits.

Example: Susan has 6 sweets. Her brother gives her 4 more. How many sweets does she have?

Model using counters to represent sweets:

Draw sketch:

Write a number sentence:

6 + 4 = 10

If children are selecting the wrong operation, provide plenty of practice using numbers under ten for all the operations. In this way you will quickly establish whether the difficulty is number based or word based.

If the child's difficulty is language based, simplify the problem by writing it in a shorter form like a telegram. Gradually help the child use their own language to reformulate the simple words into more complex language.

Example: There were three ponds on a farm. One day some ducks flew in and two ducks landed on each pond. How many ducks flew in altogether?

This can be simplified to: Three ponds with two ducks on each pond.

Give children considerable practice in rewriting problems in a simpler form as well as expanding short sentences into longer forms. This can be done orally or written down by the child or by the teacher.

If the child's difficulty is number based, then return to practising the pure number operations before returning to further word problem work. At first use small numbers and easy calculations in the word problems. When the child's confidence increases, gradually introduce more complex numbers into the word problems.

If children consistently misapply the operation required, label the different types of word problems explicitly. (They are listed in the box below.) Work on one type of word problem, talking about the features of that type of problem. Discuss how addition problems can be 'combine problems' because they involve two or more groups being put together to create one new group. Once children can talk about this easily then work on a different type of problem. Addition problems can also be 'change problems' where items are added to an initial quantity to enlarge it. When they manage addition 'change' problems successfully, give them a selection of 'combine' and 'change' problems. Make sure they identify what type of problem a question is, before they start solving it. Children can learn to recognize problems as similar to ones they may have seen before (Askew, 2004).

Gradually develop this approach to cover the types of word problems for subtraction, multiplication and division.

Children will need plenty of appropriate examples that demonstrate the different operations clearly. A good source of word problems is *BEAM's Big Book of Word Problems* by Mike Askew (2004).

Types of word problems

Word problems can be classified into categories which children can learn to recognize as similar to ones they may have seen before. (Askew, 2004)

The categories are:

- combine, change and compare for addition and subtraction
- repeated addition and the array and area models for multiplication
- grouping and sharing models for division.

Addition

- **Combine:** 2 groups put together to create 1 new group.
- **Change:** Increase an initial quantity to change it by adding items.

Subtraction

- **Change:** Decrease an initial quantity to change it by subtracting items.
- **Compare:** 2 groups are compared by finding the difference between the two groups.

Multiplication

- **Repeated addition:** Several same-sized groups can be added together.
- **Array model:** Objects are arranged in rows and columns to create a rectangle.
- **Area model:** Unit squares replace the counters in the array.

Division

- **Grouping:** The quantity in each group is known. The number of groups is unknown. (The grouping model links directly with multiplication.)
- **Sharing:** The number of groups is known. The quantity of items in each group is unknown. The answer is found by sharing the items equally between the groups.

Children working on multiplication and division word problems may become confused between the concepts of grouping and sharing. Work extensively on grouping-type word problems at first. Only when children can handle grouping problems confidently and successfully can you move on to working on sharing-type word problems.

Children with weak numeracy usually find grouping problems easier than sharing problems because it is easier to relate multiplication facts directly to the concept of grouping. For example, if 5 fours are 20 then there must be 5 fours in 20 and 4 fives in 20. The concept of sharing does not link into multiplication in such a direct or easy to understand way.

Example of a grouping problem: I have 20 biscuits. I want to give them to 4 children. How many biscuits will each child get?

In this example the size of the groups is known (5 in each group) but the number of groups is unknown. The problem can be solved by building up groups of 5 to reach 20. When all the biscuits have been put out, there will be four plates of biscuits.

Example of a sharing problem: I have 20 biscuits. I want to give them to 4 children. How many biscuits will each child get? In this example the number of groups is known (4 children) but the number in each group is unknown.

The problem can be solved by sharing the 20 biscuits between the 4 children. Each child will get 5 biscuits because there are four groups of five in 20.

At first children may revert to the nursery method of sharing 'one for me and one for you' and so on. Allow them to do this. Gradually, they will find that it is quicker to try to estimate how many items each person will receive by sharing out a certain number for each, and then adjusting their estimate according to the items remaining.

Section 6: Formal written numeracy

- Check that the child can set out and use the standard written form correctly.
- Train the child to do a rough estimation to establish the approximate size of the answer to all calculations before doing the formal written work.

Addition and subtraction

This section investigates the child's ability to use written column arithmetic.

Algorithms should be set out showing the working so that it is clear which numbers are carried or decomposed.

They should also understand that they have added (or subtracted) two-digit numbers (or more). If they can set out the digits in columns, it demonstrates some awareness of the importance of where the digit is placed, that is, of place value.

Example:

1. Shows how ten is carried into the tens column.

$$\begin{array}{r} 36 \\ 25\ + \\ \hline 6\ 1 \\ 1 \end{array}$$

2. Shows decomposition of 34 into 2 tens and 14.

$$\begin{array}{r} ^2\cancel{3}^{1}4 \\ 26\ - \\ \hline 8 \end{array}$$

3. Use of the informal method of partitioning. Each number is partitioned into tens and units. The tens are added and the units are added. Finally, they are combined to reach the answer.

$$\begin{array}{r} 36 \\ 25\ + \\ \hline 30 + 6 \\ 20 + 5 \\ \hline 50 + 11 = 61 \end{array}$$

Problems include the following:

- Inability to set out the question correctly indicates lack of understanding of the importance of the position of the digits.
- Adding rows not columns. The child does not understand place value – that 35 represents 3 tens and 5 units and 47 is four tens and 7 units. They are probably muddling up informal horizontal methods with formal written methods.

$$\begin{array}{rr} 35 & = 8 \\ 47\ + & = 11 \\ \hline & 19 \end{array}$$

- Failure to understand how to exchange. In this example the child does not realize that the one ten must be 'carried' into the tens column. Here the child has added 5 and 7, written down 12, and then added 3 and 4 to make 7. The child does not understand that the 3 and 4 represent 30 and 40 making 70 which must be added to 12 to make 82. If a child has no sense of the size of numbers, they do not realize that this answer is unreasonable.

$$\begin{array}{r} 35 \\ 47\ + \\ \hline 712 \end{array}$$

- Taking smaller number from larger number – wherever it is. Here the child has taken 4 from 7 because they have learnt to always take the smaller number from the larger number. They see each digit as a separate entity not as a part of a two-digit number.

$$\begin{array}{r} 64 \\ 17\ - \\ \hline 53 \end{array}$$

Teaching plan: *estimation; concrete representations; explain workings; spatial difficulties; principle of exchange; place value*

Train the child to do a rough estimate for all calculations before doing the formal written work. This will establish the approximate size of the answer. This will help alert them to any mistakes in the written procedure. In the example above, 35 + 47 will be rounded up to 40 + 50. This equals 90, so the answer of 712 is impossible.

It is essential to use concrete materials to investigate how numbers are constructed from tens and ones and how one ten can be exchanged for ten ones.

For addition, the child should build the numbers on a place-value grid using base ten materials and combine them doing appropriate exchanges where necessary. Encourage them to explain exactly what they are doing. They should write the question in the standard form and record the steps as they do them.

For subtraction, the child should build the larger number on the place-value grid and practise solving the problem by removing the amount representing the smaller number. They should be trained to subtract the units (doing any exchange if necessary) before subtracting the quantities in the tens position. They should write the question in the standard form and record the steps as they do them.

If a child is unable to set out a sum independently, analyse why they find it difficult. Is it because they have a problem setting their work out on the page? Is it because they are working on squared paper? Is it because they do not understand the importance of placing units under units and tens under tens? Is it because they are having difficulty writing down or remembering what has been said to them? Is it because they are having trouble copying what the teacher has written in a different format? Some of these difficulties may be caused by underlying problems. (See discussion of co-morbid conditions in Chapter 1, page 1.)

If the child has difficulties writing the numbers in columns write HTU above the columns. Write each letter in a different colour to draw attention to the columns. Use the same colours in every lesson.

Most children are helped by working on squared paper. However, those with visual spatial difficulties or dyspraxic tendencies may initially prefer to work on unlined paper which they could find less distracting.

Children who have trouble writing units under units and tens under tens may not understand the importance of the position of the digits in a number. They may need to work on understanding place value.

Children with handwriting difficulties can have problems writing down what is dictated to them. If so, the teacher can write down the questions or the numbers for them, leaving them free to concentrate on finding the answer and writing that down. Others with weak memories might find it difficult to remember what has been said to them. They should be encouraged to repeat back the question before solving it. If this difficulty persists, the teacher should write the question down for them and make sure that they can read it. Never mind if it is in words or digits.

Many children with visual memory weaknesses will have trouble either copying from a board or from a worksheet or textbook. Simplify the task by providing worksheets and making sure that they are visually uncluttered; that is, they are clearly set out with plenty of white space between items.

In column arithmetic, if children are adding the digits in the rows rather than the columns, provide visual reminders. Write HTU above the columns and draw vertical lines in a colour between the letters HTU demarcating the columns. Give plenty of simple examples without exchange before explicitly teaching it.

Teaching addition involving exchange

If children do not understand why quantities are carried from one column to another, return to working on the principle of exchange. Use the place-value grid and base ten material or the Stern dual board to demonstrate the principle. (If a child has been taught to record exchanges in a way that is working for them, do not attempt to change it as long as they can explain what they are doing.)

It is essential that the child demonstrates why the algorithm 'works' by doing the steps concretely on a place-value grid and writing it alongside. This is particularly important for children with low numeracy or children who appear to be just following a recipe. Remember to make sure that they talk about what they are doing.

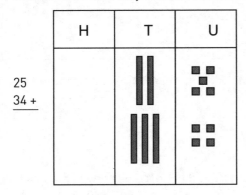

1. Set out sum.   2. Combine quantities to reach the total.

Teaching subtraction involving exchange

If children are taking the smaller digit from the larger digit in the numbers, they do not understand that each horizontally written number represents a whole number. They may not understand that the value of the digit depends on its place in the number. Return to place-value work, building up numbers using concrete materials.

Next, teach formal subtraction by using concrete materials alongside the written algorithm.

Example: 64 – 17

Train the child to explain in their own words what they are going to do. 'I am going to take 17 away from 64'. They build the number 64 but do not build the number 17.

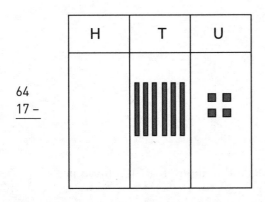

1. Set out sum.   2. Exchange 1 ten for 10 ones.

If the child tries to start by taking one ten away from the 6 tens, then teach them the mantra 'You must start with the units'. When the child attempts to take 7 ones away from the 4 ones on the grid they will realize this is not possible. This moment provides the opportunity to teach decomposition. Exchange one ten for ten ones and place them in the unit column with the four units already there. The child will then see that it is now possible to take seven away from the 14 units in the units column. They may do it by removing them one by one. However, encourage them to place the units in the dot patterns of 10 and 4 which will make it easier to remove them in a more systematic way than one by one.

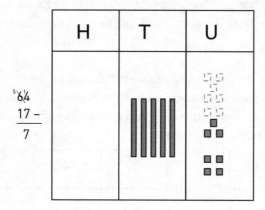

3. Remove 7 ones from the units column.

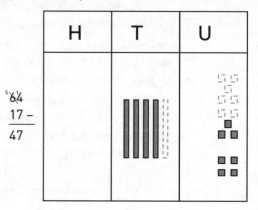

4. Finally remove 1 ten from the tens column.

Written multiplication

The formal written multiplication method should be correctly and appropriately used.

The child should be able to demonstrate that they understand how to apply the principle of exchange.

However, first it checks children's understanding of multiplication. Many schools now only teach up to 10 times in a table. It is useful to check if children understand that 11×6 would be one six more than 10×6 and that 12×6 would be two more sixes. If children do know up to 12 times in a table, those with poor understanding remain adamant they can go no further. It is important to work with them until they are confident they can work out harder facts beyond their limits of knowledge.

The child may prefer to use a Simple Box Method of multiplication.
Example: 23×15

Simple Box Method

×	10	5
20	200	100
3	30	15

$23 \times 15 = 200 + 100 + 30 + 15$
$= 300 + 45$
$= 345$

Problems:
- If the child has to use the formal method to multiply by 10, this indicates they do not understand place value.
- If the child works this out using repeated addition they may not understand place value ($23 + 23 + 23 + 23 + 23 + 23 + 23 + 23 + 23 + 23$).

$$\begin{array}{r} 23 \\ 10 \times \\ \hline 00 \\ 230 \\ \hline 230 \end{array}$$

- The child has multiplied 1 × 100, written that down, then multiplied 4 × 100 and written that alongside. They certainly do not have a sense of the size of the numbers they are dealing with because they do not realize that the answer is totally unrealistic.

$$\begin{array}{r} 41 \\ 100 \times \\ \hline 400100 \end{array}$$

- The child is either muddling up formal and informal methods, or muddling up rows and columns. Some children who have been taught but not understood a Simple Box Method deal with formal multiplication in this way. They do not understand place value. They have multiplied 2 × 3 and 1 × 5 and then put the two digits together to get 65.

$$\begin{array}{r} 23 = 6 \\ 15 \times\ = 5 \\ \hline 65 \end{array}$$

- The child has multiplied 7 × 4 to get 28 but does not know how to deal with the tens number that is carried over so they write 28. Next, they multiply 2 × 4 and write the 8 next to the 28. Two possible explanations are the child may not understand the place-value system, or they may not understand the principle of exchange.

$$\begin{array}{r} 27 \\ 4 \times \\ \hline 828 \end{array}$$

Teaching plan: *estimation; extending tables facts; revise place value*

Multiplying larger numbers

Teach the child to make a rough estimate of the expected answer before starting any calculation. This will alert them to any errors in the calculation if they have made mistakes in the procedure as in the examples of problems above. Example: 13 × 6 is approximately 10 × 6 = 60, therefore the answer must be more than 60.

23 × 15 can be rounded to 20 × 20, which is 400. Some children may be able to manage a closer estimation by multiplying 20 × 15 to give 300. The answer will be a bit bigger.

If the child has selected an appropriate and efficient method such as calculating from a known fact, this strategy can be encouraged and developed. (Example: 13 × 6 'I know 10 × 6 = 60 therefore 13 × 6 must be three more sixes. 3 × 6 = 18, so 13 × 6 will be 60 plus 18'.)

However, if the child is unable to work out the answer to 13 × 6 they will need to be taught how to extend key tables facts to larger numbers outside the table. If the child cannot derive their answers from previously known facts, work on linking the two. Use concrete materials and make sure that the child talks about what they are doing.

Example: 13 × 6

The child uses counters to lay out a row of 10 sixes.

Discuss the fact that you need 3 more sixes to make 13 sixes altogether.

10 × 6 = 60 and 3 × 6 = 18. The answer is found by adding 60 and 18.

Formal written methods

If the child has to write a formal sum to multiply by 10, this shows they do not understand the number system. Teaching will need to return to place-value work.

Children who show error patterns that indicate they do not understand place value and the principle of exchange are not ready to use formal written methods of multiplication. Robert Ashlock (2006) discusses multiplication errors in detail in *Error Patterns in Computation*. Return to teaching place-value work and the concept of multiplication.

Written division

Children should solve division problems with reference to multiplication facts. They should understand the concept of remainders.

Dividing by 1, 100, or 1000: How the child deals with dividing 140 by 10 will indicate whether they are merely carrying out a procedure or whether they understand the concept of division. Many children have learnt to cross out the final zero to reach the answer 14 without understanding what this means. Some children sketch a form of place-value grid and have been taught to derive their answers by moving digits on a place-value grid to solve these kinds of problems. The child who can reason that since 14 tens make 140 there must be 14 tens in 140 is likely to have a better understanding of the concept of division.

Short division: The child should understand that the question is asking how many fives there are in 45. They may solve it by setting it out formally or they may solve it by relating it to multiplication. When dealing with remainders they should be able to explain what their answer means.

Example: $6\overline{)25}$

The child should say: 'The answer is 4 remainder 1 because 4 sixes make 24 so there will be one left over'.

Teaching plan: *estimation; linking multiplication and division; remainders; arrays and the area model*

If children are not solving division problems with reference to multiplication facts, develop this skill by pointing out and discussing the direct links between multiplication and division. Help children develop a strong visual image of the concept by using concrete materials to demonstrate this and link it to the formal written method.

Demonstrating 3 fours using Cuisenaire rods and an array.

In division the child should understand the concept of remainders. If they are unsure about this, do plenty of worked examples with concrete materials and record the results. Ask the child to make up word problems and use concrete materials to support their thinking. The next stage is to draw diagrams or drawings to illustrate the problem before setting it out in written form.

If the child is not able to deal with short division orally, work on consolidating simple division by using counters and talking about the process as they do it. If they succeed with the oral part, teach them how to record their oral solutions formally.

Example: $6\overline{)25}$

○○○○○○○○○○ ○○○○○○○○○○ ○○○○○

Count out 25 counters.

Now put them in an array with six rows.
It is clear that 25 ÷ 6 will be 4 remainder 1 which consists of 6 rows with 4 in each row and 1 left over.
This structure clearly links to the formal written division.

Note

1. Orthoptists work diagnosing and treating congenital or acquired anomalies of vision, focusing and visuo-motor functions. Behavioural optometrists use lenses and vision training to facilitate the development of a more efficient and complete visual process.

Games and activities

Number sense and counting

The games in this section introduce the concept of number. The structure of the counting system is introduced, as well as the idea that numbers can be used to compare quantities.

Children need to learn to say the number names in order. They need to understand the principle of one-to-one correspondence, which is that the numbers in the count are synchronized with each object being counted. They also need to understand that when they have counted a number of items, the last number mentioned represents how many there are in that group. Children also need to learn the ordinal numbers; that is, the numbers representing the place in a sequence such as first, second, third.

Estimating skills are essential, particularly for children with low numeracy. This is especially true in the technological age when you need to be able to recognize whether a computer-generated calculation is sensible. The Estimating Game gives children practice in improving their judgement of quantities. It will also help the child to develop a feel for the relative size of numbers as well as giving practice in counting.

Oral counting is the ability to recite the number sequence. Children should be able to do this with accuracy and reasonable fluency.

Reading and writing numbers are implicit in most of the games in this chapter as children record scores and talk about what they are doing.

Calculation

Children need to be able to perform calculations on numbers by applying the four operations – addition, subtraction, multiplication and division. To do this efficiently they need to know key number facts: doubles and near doubles bonds, bonds of ten, and the 10 times table. The other number facts can be derived from the key facts by reasoning. However, it is helpful if some of these additional facts can also be learnt.

The dot patterns help to develop pattern recognition and an awareness of the relative sizes of the counting numbers 1 to 9. These patterns make it clear that all quantities greater than one are made from smaller quantities. The dot patterns also help children learn important number bonds.

Place value

Children need to be able to recognize and generate numbers greater than 10. They need to understand how numbers are ordered into hundreds, tens and units in the number system. They should understand the relationships between the numbers before they can work reliably with them.

Early recording systems, such as tally marks, showed one symbol for each item counted. The idea of using 'place' to show value requires a step into the abstract. Understanding the concept is difficult for many children because it is an invented convention.

Pupils need to understand that you can exchange several items for one of greater value. This is fundamental to understanding the place-value system. Money can help to establish this, but children need to work with concrete objects.

Multiplication and division

Knowing the multiplication tables 'off by heart' is a great help in calculation. However, some children are not able to remember them all. They should learn the key tables of 10 times a number and 5 times a number and be able to derive all the tables facts from these.

It will be easier for children to learn the times tables if they develop a 'feel' for multiplication and division by understanding how they are related to each other and what they represent in concrete terms.

Equipment and how to use it

Base ten material

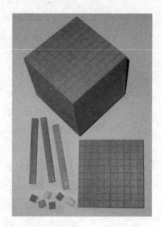

Equipment: 1 cm³ cubes, ten rods, 100 squares, 1000 cube, tape measure.

The base ten material consists of wooden cubes and cuboids for learning about the tens-based system. It also encapsulates the links among length, area and volume.

The unit cube is 1 cm³, the tens rod is 10 cm long, the 100 square is 10 cm × 10 cm, and the 1000 cube is 10 cm × 10 cm × 10 cm.

Some children will use the equipment and name it correctly but do not really understand what the sizes represent. Children should be allowed to play with the equipment as well as doing structured activities to investigate the relationships and prove to themselves that there actually are 100 small cubes in the 100 square and 1000 small cubes in the 1000 cube. Children often express surprise when they have done these activities.

Prove it is true

Activity 1. Measure the ten rod using 1 cm³ by placing ten 1 cm³ cubes next to it to prove that there are ten ones in one tens rod

Activity 2. Check how many 1 cm³ in a 100 square*
- Count 1 cm³ onto the 100 square.
- Count them to check that a 100 square is made of 100 small cubes.
- Count the 100 cubes of 1 cm³ each into a line.*
- Use a tape measure to measure the line of cubes.

Activity 3. Check how many 1 cm³ in a 1000 cube*
- Place the 1000 cube on the table.
- Build another 1000 next to it using 1 cm³ cubes to prove that the cube actually does contain 1000 cubes of 1 cm³ each.
- Count the 1000 cubes of 1 cm³ each into a line.
- Use a tape measure to measure the line of cubes.

* Children who have already mastered the principle of exchange may decide to exchange the ones for ten rods to make it quicker. Allow them to do so but do not suggest they do so. The children who continue to use the 1 cm³ cubes do so because they have not understood the concept yet. Putting out the individual cubes will help them realize that there must be a quicker way of doing this.

Cuisenaire rods

Cuisenaire rods are coloured cuboids where different colours represent the numbers 1 to 10. Initially, children should play with the rods, name the colours and explore the relationships between them. They can be used in structured ways for comparing and sequencing numbers, for adding, subtracting, multiplying and dividing, and later for fraction work.

Exploring Cuisenaire rods

Children can discover the length of each rod by measuring them with the white ones.

They can build flat designs on 1 cm² paper, copy sequences, and copy designs with rods or by drawing.

Relative sizes of number

In sequencing quantities you need to understand how each number is related to the number next to it. The Cuisenaire rods provide a structured way of exploring the counting numbers. Children should be allowed to play with them to explore the relationships between the rods and work out what they represent.

The Staircase Game uses Cuisenaire rods to introduce the sequence of the counting numbers up to 10.

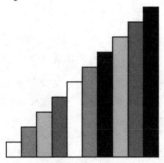

Cuisenaire-rod staircase showing how each rod differs by one.

Making number patterns

Cuisenaire rods provide a strong visual image of the bonds within numbers. By making rod 'sandwiches' children can clearly see the various combinations that can be combined to make another number.

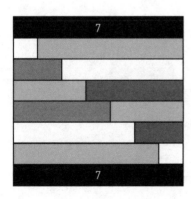

Bonds of 7

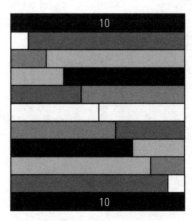

Bonds of ten

Stern blocks

Number squares and the dual board

Stern equipment is similar to Cuisenaire rods in that it consists of different coloured wooden cubes and cuboids that are related to each other by size. The advantage of the Cuisenaire rods is that they are based on the metric unit of 1 cm³. The advantage of the Stern equipment is that the pieces are larger, making it easier for small children to handle and the individual units are marked on each piece. The Stern equipment also has square base boards for each of the numbers 1 to 9 and the dual board for teaching the principle of exchange and place value.

The principle of exchange on the dual board

The dual board makes the link between tens and units explicit. It consists of a square frame with a space for 10 tens blocks. To the right is the units column with a space for 10 unit cubes. The top space in the units column has an arrow pointing to the tens column.

The child counts ones into the units column. Before they place the tenth unit to cover up the arrow they should say: 'When I have ten ones I exchange them for one ten'. Then the child can place one ten on the frame next to the units to do the exchange, remove the units and put the ten into the tens column. Child says: 'Now I have 1 ten'. The child then counts another group of ones into the units column. They will then see that this produces 2 tens which makes 20.

Stern blocks

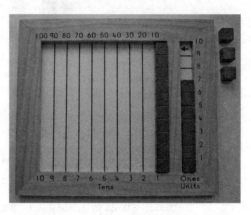

Stern dual board

Activities

Discovering dot patterns

Children need visual images of the size of numbers. They need to develop the concept of relative size and to think in terms of components.

Dot patterns:

- enable visualization of quantities
- show that all quantities greater than 1 are made up of smaller quantities
- help with bonds.

Developing dot patterns

Ask the pupil to use counters to put out patterns for numbers up to 6.

Explain that you want to make patterns that are easy to recognize and compare.

Suggest that they use the dice pattern if they do not want to experiment.

If the pupil does want to experiment, let them enjoy exploring, then discuss their patterns and suggest they see what other patterns they can make. Do not dismiss their patterns but also show them the dice patterns (shown below) and discuss the ways in which smaller numbers are combined to make the larger numbers. These forms are visually distinctive.

Discuss the composition of the various patterns drawing attention to the doubles. (You may wish to use the opportunity to introduce the vocabulary associated with the concept of doubling – halving, twice, etc. – as well as the concept of a group.)

Ask the pupil if they can make a pattern that is double 4 and another that is double 5, so that if someone else looks at it they can see immediately that it is made from the 4 pattern, or the 5 pattern.

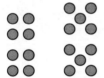

Ask them to put the patterns in order. Do they notice anything missing? If they do not realize that 7 and 9 are 'missing' do not tell them. You will need to encourage them to explore and find out for themselves. However, it is an indication that the pupil has little idea of the concept of number and will have to be very carefully taught before they can progress in maths.

Next, discuss the patterns that are one *more than*, or one *less than* a double.

Now ask them to make a pattern that is one more than 8 but one less than 10. Explore both ways of making this; that is, make the pattern for 10 and remove one counter, then make the pattern for 8 and add one counter.

Finally, make the pattern for 7. There are various options but try to encourage the pupil to use the 4 and 3 pattern.

Bonds of ten

Pupils need to be able to recognize and generate the bonds of ten. This is absolutely essential.

Prerequisite – sequencing numbers to 10

Use cubes to investigate the way that each number is one more, or one less, than the number adjacent to it. Build a 'staircase' using Cuisenaire rods.

Concrete investigation

Use Cuisenaire rods to explore all the different ways you can make 10 by combining two rods.

Build two 'staircases' using rods and slot them together so that they form a rod 'sandwich' in which each row is equal to 10.

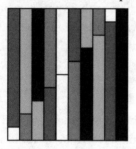   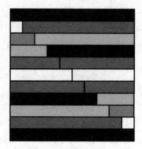

A Cuisenaire-rod 'stair-case' showing bonds of ten

A Cuisenaire-rod 'sandwich' showing bonds of ten

Use counters to make the core patterns and see which patterns you need to combine to make 10.

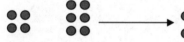

$4 + 6 = 10$

From concrete to abstract: triads

Triads are a way of representing number bonds in a written form which emphasises the relationship between the numbers.

Example: $10 = 1 + 9$

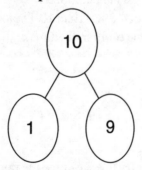

Here the number sentences are only concerned with reading the triad from 10 at the top.

This represents
$$10 = 9 + 1$$
$$10 = 1 + 9$$
$$10 - 1 = 9$$
$$10 - 9 = 1$$

Place value: building numbers

Start building work by naming the value of base ten material. For example, 'Can you make a number with 3 tens and 5 units or 2 hundreds, 4 tens and 1 unit?'

Always ensure that children can do the following.

1. Make designated numbers from base ten material and then record them, e.g. 'Can you make the number 35 for me?'

   'Now can you write the number you made for me?'

2. Read a number from base ten and then *record* it, e.g. 'What is this number I've made for you? Can you write the number I have made?'

3. Read the written abstract form of a number and build it from base ten material, e.g. 'Can you tell me what this number is? (Teacher writes 35.) Can you make it for me using some of these tens and some of these units?'

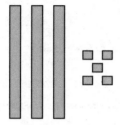

Base ten material used to show that 3 tens and 5 units = 35

The games in the place value section are designed to practise the principle of exchange and decomposing numbers. They also provide a strong visual image of the concept of place value.

Multiplication: the times tables strategy

Work on one table at a time.

1. **Develop children's understanding of the concepts of multiplication and division.**
   - Practise step-counting.
   - Extend children's step-counting skills so they become used to thinking in 'steps' or groups.
   - Build multiplication and division relationships as repeated groups using concrete materials to create strong visual images.
   - Build multiplication and division relationships as arrays and area models.
   - Ensure the child talks about what they are doing and the relationships between the numbers.
   - Work on multiplication and division word problems.

2. **Develop children's knowledge of the times tables sequences. Teach children to use a simple universal tables strategy.**
   - Learn the key fact $10 \times n$ and revise repeatedly.
   - Derive $5 \times n$ by reasoning from $10 \times n$ [5 is half of 10 therefore $5 \times n$ will be half of $10 \times n$].
   - Learn the key fact $5 \times n$ and revise repeatedly.
   - Reason from key tables facts to figure out other tables facts.
   - Practice using the key facts frequently. With practice children reason increasingly efficiently, and more and more tables are known 'by heart'.

Example for the ×3 table:

Key facts: $1 \times 3 = 3$ $5 \times 3 = 15$ $10 \times 3 = 30$

Other tables facts are derived by reasoning or step-counting from the key facts.

To work out 7×3 the child reasons: $5 \times 3 = 15$. Seven is two more than 5 so I need to add two more groups of three which is six. So 7×3 will be $15 + 6$ which makes 21 [$7 \times 3 = (5 \times 3) + 3 + 3$ or use step-counting 15, 18, 21].

To work out 9×3 the child reasons from 10×3. The child says: $10 \times 3 = 30$. I know 9×3 is one less three. Therefore, 9×3 is $30 - 3 = 27$.

Summary
- The key tables facts $10 \times n$ and $5 \times n$ must be known 'by heart'.
- Children have to practise figuring out other facts using efficient reasoning routes.

Games

Number sense and counting

THE ESTIMATING GAME

Aims
* To introduce the idea of the structured number track.
* To develop the concept of the size of numbers.

Equipment
* Counters – between 10 and 50. (If you don't have counters, use any small objects such as coins or dried beans.)
* A sheet of paper to cover the objects.
* Score sheet and pencil. (See layout below.)

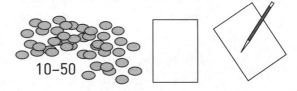

10–50

How to play
Scatter a handful of objects on the table. Allow a few seconds to look at them *but not long enough to count them*. (You will need to experiment to find a satisfactory length of time. Start by allowing 5 seconds and make the time shorter as players improve.)

Cover the objects with a sheet of paper.

Player 1 says what their estimate of the number of objects is. Everyone records this on their score sheet. Each player gives an estimate. All are recorded.

Player 1 counts the actual number of objects and puts them out in a single line, counting aloud and leaving a gap between each group of 10.

Everyone records the total in the 'Actual Number' column.

The winner is the player whose estimate is closest to the actual number of objects. Enter the winner's name in the appropriate column.

Example showing play:

 Counters are scattered.

Players write their estimates.

| | Estimate of Number | | | | Actual | |
	Player 1	Player 2	Player 3	Player 4	Number	Winner
Game 1	23	31	22	29		
Game 2						
Game 3						

Player 1 puts counters into groups of 10 in a single line and counts them.

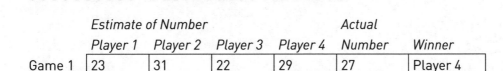

| | Estimate of Number | | | | Actual | |
	Player 1	Player 2	Player 3	Player 4	Number	Winner
Game 1	23	31	22	29	27	Player 4

Player 4 wins Game 1.

CATERPILLAR TRACKS

Aims
- To reinforce the importance of the base ten structure.
- To compare quantities.

Equipment
- Counters – 20 for each player
- 1–3 spinner or number 1–6 dice (depending on age of pupil)
- Board with one 'track' for each player

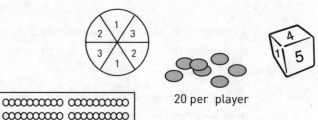

20 per player

How to play
Players take turns to spin or roll a number and take the quantity of counters indicated. Each time, the player places the quantity of counters 'earned' on their own track.

On each turn, players should say the number represented by their running total quantities. (Note: Players should be encouraged to say how close or distant individual quantities are to the decade numbers that they lie between.)

The winner is the first player to cover the length of their track.

Example showing play:
Empty tracks

ⵔⵔⵔⵔⵔⵔⵔⵔⵔⵔ ⵔⵔⵔⵔⵔⵔⵔⵔⵔⵔ
ⵔⵔⵔⵔⵔⵔⵔⵔⵔⵔ ⵔⵔⵔⵔⵔⵔⵔⵔⵔⵔ

Round 1: Player A throws 4, Player B throws 3

●●●●ⵔⵔⵔⵔⵔⵔ ⵔⵔⵔⵔⵔⵔⵔⵔⵔⵔ   Player A
●●●ⵔⵔⵔⵔⵔⵔⵔ ⵔⵔⵔⵔⵔⵔⵔⵔⵔⵔ   Player B

Round 2: Player A throws 2, Player B throws 6

●●●●●●ⵔⵔⵔⵔ ⵔⵔⵔⵔⵔⵔⵔⵔⵔⵔ   Player A
●●●●●●●●●ⵔ ⵔⵔⵔⵔⵔⵔⵔⵔⵔⵔ   Player B

Player A says: 'I have 6 counters'.
Player B says: 'I have 9 counters'.

UNTANGLING -TEEN AND -TY

Aim
- Distinguish between the word-endings '-teen' and '-ty'.

Equipment
- Pencil and paper
- Base sheet with two columns headed -teen and -ty
- -teen and -ty cards

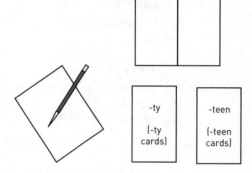

The teen cards have the numbers 13 to 19 on one side. Write the suffix -teen on the back of each. The -ty cards have the multiples of ten from 20 to 90. Write the suffix -ty on the back of these.

For confident players use cards with -teen and -ty numbers in the hundreds.

How to play
Player A holds the cards with the number side up. Read each number, emphasizing the ending and place the card in the correct column. When all the cards have been played the player turns the cards over and checks that they are correct.

Score 1 for each incorrect answer.

Player B has a turn.

The winner is the person with the lowest score.

-teen	-ty
13	30

THE STAIRCASE GAME

Aims
- To build a sequence using Cuisenaire rods.
- To develop the concept of comparison.
- To develop a strong visual image of comparative size.

Equipment
- Cuisenaire rods*
- 1–10 dice

How to play
First player throws the dice and takes the matching Cuisenaire rod.

Second player has a turn.

If a player throws a number they have already taken, they miss a turn.

The winner is the first person to build a sequence of 4 rods.

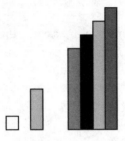

A winning sequence: 6, 7, 8, 9.

The player wins with 6, 7, 8, 9. They have also thrown 1 and 3 during the game and placed these in the correct positions.

   (The game can be continued by playing the first to get 5 rods in sequence. For a longer version play the first to get 10 rods in a row.)

* If you do not have Cuisenaire rods, use base ten cubes. The staircase will then look like this:

FOUR IN ORDER

(Putting number patterns in the correct sequence.)

Aims
- To recognize number patterns.
- To sequence numbers.

Equipment
- Pattern cards 1–10 (one set for each player)
- 1–10 dice

How to play

Place the pattern cards randomly, face up, in the middle of the table.

First player throws the dice and takes the pattern card that matches the number thrown. They place the card in front of them.

The second player has a turn.

Players take turns collecting cards. The cards should be placed in sequence in a row in front of each player.

If a player throws a number they have already taken, they miss a turn.

The winner is the first person to get a sequence of four consecutive numbers.

Cards in play:

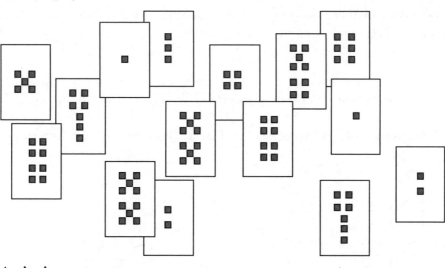

A winning sequence:

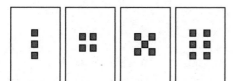

Calculation

PATTERN PAIRS

(A matching and memory game.)

Aims
- To learn to recognize numbers.
- To develop a strong visual image of the core patterns.
- To develop concentration.

Equipment
- Number cards 1–10
- Pattern cards 1–10
- Word cards one–ten

(Each set of cards should be a different colour. If there are three or more players use two packs of each set of cards.)

How to play

Game A (pattern cards and number cards): Spread all the pattern cards and number cards, face down, on the table.

The first player turns up a pattern card. They read the number aloud and say which number they are looking for. They turn up a number card. If they are a matching pair they keep them and have another turn.

If the player does not find a matching pair, they turn the cards face down. It is very important that cards always remain in the same position on the table.

The next player has a turn.

The winner is the person with the most pairs when all the cards have been collected.

Game B (pattern cards and word cards): Play as above but use the pattern cards and word cards.

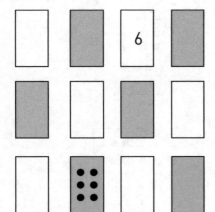

SHUT THE BOX

Aims
- To learn the dot patterns.
- To practise number bonds.

Equipment
- Number cards 1–10 (one set for each player)
- Spinner and pattern underlay
- Score sheet

Number cards (1–10)

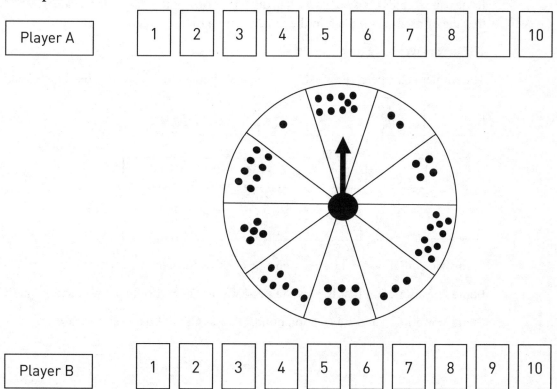

How to play

Place playing cards in sequence, face up.

First player spins the spinner and turns over a card with the same number as the dot pattern.

Second player has a turn.

If a player spins a number that has already been turned over, they miss a turn.*

The winner is the first player to Shut the Box by turning over all their cards.

Example:

Player A		1	2	3	4	5	6	7	8		10

Player B		1	2	3	4	5	6	7	8	9	10

Player B wins the game.

---

* For a more advanced game a player can turn over two cards that 'make' the number spun. This can be done using addition or subtraction bonds. Example: Spin 7 and you can turn over 5 and 2, 6 and 1, 4 and 3, or 4, 2 and 1. (You must use all the components of the number.) Or you could turn over 1 and 8, 2 and 9, or 3 and 10 because 10 minus 3, 9 minus 2 or 8 minus 1 equal 7.

BONDS OF TEN PAIRS

Aims
- To practise bonds of ten.
- To introduce the missing addend (the first step to learning subtraction).

$3 + \boxed{} = 10$ $\boxed{7}$

$10 - 6 =$ $\boxed{4}$

(answer cards)

Equipment
- 1 set of addition question cards (e.g. $3 + \square = 10$)
- 1 set of subtraction question cards (e.g. $10 - 6 = \square$)
- 2 sets of number cards 0–9

How to play

Game 1: Spread the addition questions cards and one set of answer cards, face down, on the table.

The first player turns up two cards, one question card and one answer card. If they make a bond of 10 they keep the pair and have another turn.

If the pair of cards does not make ten, the player turns them face down again. (Note: It is essential that the cards always remain in the same position on the table.)

The next player has a turn.

The winner is the person with the most cards when all the cards have been collected.

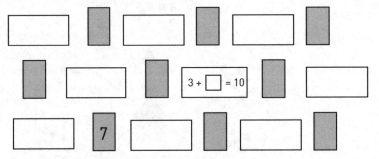

Cards laid out for play with a winning pair of cards turned up.

Game 2: Subtraction bonds. Play the same way as Game 1 but use subtraction question cards.

Game 3: Addition and subtraction bonds. Play as Game 1 using all the cards.

CLEAR THE DECK

(Based on the game 'Clear the Deck' in Butterworth and Yeo 2004.)

Aim

* To practise bonds of ten.

Equipment

* Number cards – 4 sets of numbers 1–9

How to play

The dealer shuffles the cards and places 12 cards, face up, in three rows.

The first player takes two cards that make 10. They do not have to be next to each other. The dealer then replaces the cards with two more. The next player has a turn.

Play continues until all the pairs of cards have been found.

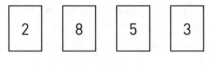

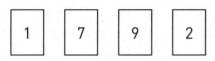

THE TINS GAME

(The Tins Game was invented by Martin Hughes, 1986.)

Aims

- To understand the concept of addition.
- To learn to count on from a number.
- To understand the commutativity principle for addition.
- To practise estimating skills.

Equipment

- Tin with a lid
- Pencil
- Labels or Post-it notes
- 20 counters (larger quantities for more able children) in a container
- Score sheet for each player

How to play

Activity: Give the player two quantities of counters, one large and one smaller one. Player counts one. The player selects which quantity to count first. They count the counters in ones into an empty tin and put the lid on. They write the number of counters on a label and stick it on top of the tin. They now add the second quantity of counters by counting on from the number on the tin.

Game (see Strategy below): Each player has three turns.

Player A takes a handful of at least five counters. They count the counters in ones into an empty tin and put the lid on. They write the number of counters on a label and stick it on top of the tin.

Player B takes at least three counters and counts them on the table. They ask player A to add them to the counters in the tin by counting on. If the answer is correct, Player A records the total. If they are incorrect, Player B asks Player A to take the counters out of the tin and count them all. Player A writes the number on the score sheet.

Now Player B has a turn.

At the end of the game the players add up their scores. The winner is the player with the highest total. A variation is for the winner to be the player with the lowest score.

6 + 5 = 11

Strategy: This game has an element of strategy in it. Each player can influence the total of the other player by the quantity that they give the other player. Since neither player is allowed to count the objects until they have taken them out of the container, they need to estimate how many they can take by feel. For this reason they are not allowed to take time in selecting the counters or they could subtly count them.

Place value

TENS AND UNITS GAME

Aim

- To understand the place-value system.

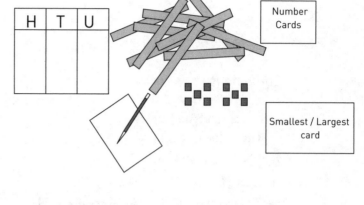

Equipment

- 4 sets of number cards 0–9
- Base ten rods and cubes
- Place-value grid for each player
- Smallest/Largest card
- Score sheet and pencil

How to play

The first player deals two cards to
each player. The dealer looks at their cards and decides whether the smallest or largest number will win. They display the 'smallest/largest' card on the appropriate side.

Each player puts their cards into the appropriate positions on the place-value grid.

They take the correct value in rods and put these on the place-value grid.

Players write their own number on the score sheet under the correct place-value headings.

Players take it in turn to read their numbers.

The player with the largest/smallest number (as decided by the dealer) gains one point.

All the cards are collected and Player 2 deals the cards. (Alternatively, the winner of each round can keep all the cards played in that round. In this case the overall winner is the person with the most cards.)

The winner is the person with the most points at the end of the game.

A game in progress: The dealer has decided that the smallest number wins, so the player makes the smaller of the two numbers they could make.

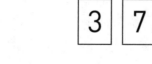

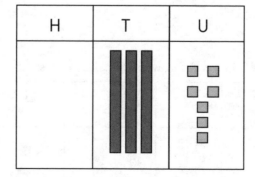

FIRST TO 30

(This game was devised by Brian Butterworth and Dorian Yeo, *Dyscalculia Guidance*.)

Aim
- To introduce concept of exchange and redistribution.

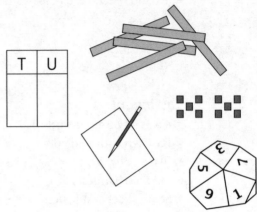

Equipment
- Dice 1–6 or 0–9
- Base ten rods and cubes
- Place-value grid for each player
- Score sheet and pencil

How to play

Each player has a basic TU place-value grid.

Players take turns to roll the dice. Dice rolls indicate the number of ones cubes which the player should take to place on their grid.

As soon as 10 or more cubes are accumulated in the units position, 10 ones must be exchanged for a ten rod and moved across to the tens position.

Each player also records a running total in headed columns.

The winner is the first person to reach 30.

Example:

Round 1: Player A throws 6 and takes 6 ones. They put out 6 ones and write the number 6 in the correct column alongside the place-value grid.

Round 2: Player A throws 5 and takes 5 ones.

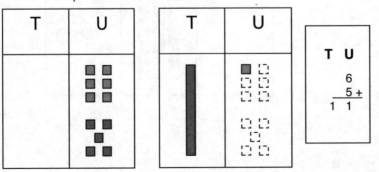

Before exchange and redistribution

After exchange and redistribution

Written recording of running total

BACK TRACK

Aim

- To practise subtraction and decomposition.

Equipment

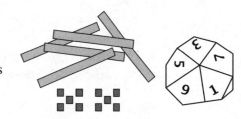

- Cuisenaire rods or base ten rods (5 tens and 10 ones for each player)
- 0–9 dice

How to play

Each player places 5 tens rods in a row.

The first player throws a dice and subtracts the number from the total.

Initially, the player must exchange one ten for 10 ones and then remove the number subtracted. More proficient players may prefer to use the Cuisenaire rods.

The winner is the first player to reach 0.

Example: Showing play after the first round.

Player 1 has thrown 8.

Player 2 has thrown 2.

Multiplication

THE MULTIPLICATION GAME

Aims
- To understand multiplication as repeated addition.
- To understand the array model of multiplication.
- To understand commutativity.
- To practise multiplication tables.

Equipment
- Paper and pencil
- Numbered dice 1–10
- Spinner with tables to be practised
- Counters all the same colour (sufficient for 10 times the highest number on the spinner)

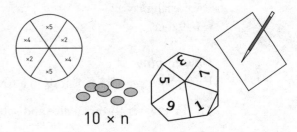

10 × n

How to play

Game 1: Player A throws the dice and spins the spinner. They say the answer either 'off by heart' or reason from the key facts. Then they put out the appropriate quantity of counters in the dot patterns. The player says what they have put out. For example, throw 3 × 5. Player says '3 fives' or '3 groups of 5 makes 15'.

Write down the score.

Player B has a turn.

The winner is the person with the highest score.

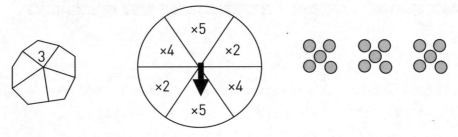

3 × 5 shown as 3 fives

Game 2: Set a target number of 100. (Vary the target number according to the size of the tables being practised.) Player A throws the dice and spins the spinner. They say the answer either 'off by heart' or reason from the key facts. They put out the appropriate quantity of counters in rows and columns. The player says what they have put out. For example, 3 × 5 Player says 3 rows with five in each row. More confident players can explore the commutativity principle either by putting out two arrays to show that 3 × 5 and 5 × 3 are the same array in different orientations, or simply by moving around the table to view the array from a different angle.

3 × 5 array   5 × 3 array

```
○ ○ ○ ○ ○                      ○ ○ ○
○ ○ ○ ○ ○                      ○ ○ ○
○ ○ ○ ○ ○                      ○ ○ ○
                               ○ ○ ○
                               ○ ○ ○
```

The winner is the person whose total is closest to the target number. If a player goes beyond the target number, they lose all their points and start again. However, any player may 'stop the clock' at any stage. When they do this each of the other players has one more turn.

FUN TIMES

(A matching and memory game.)

Aim
- To practise times tables.
- To improve memory.

Equipment
- Times table question cards
- Times table answer cards

5 × 6	**30**

(Each set of cards should be a different colour.)

How to play

Spread all the cards, face down, on the table.

The first player turns up a question card. They read the table question and say what they are looking for. (Talking about the cards is an essential part of this game. The players should also stop occasionally and say which cards have been turned up, what they are and who turned them up, without turning them up.) Example: Turns up 5 × 6. Says 'Five sixes are 30 so I am looking for 30'.

They turn up an answer card. If they are a matching pair, they keep them and have another turn.

If the player does not find a matching pair, they read the number on the answer card and say what multiplication makes that number. Example: Looking for 30 turns up 48. They say, '48 is made of 8 sixes'.

If the player does not find a matching pair, they turn the cards face down. It is very important that cards always remain in the same position on the table.

The next player has a turn.

The winner is the person with the most pairs when all the cards have been collected.

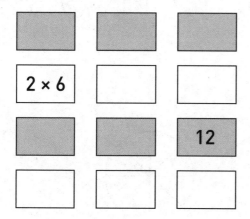

SPIN AND TRACK

Aims
- To practise exchanging ten ones for one ten.
- To explore the difference between addition and multiplication.
- To practise addition and multiplication.

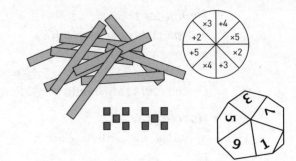

Equipment
- 1 dice 1–10
- 1 spinner × 2, 3, 4, 5 and + 2, 3, 4, 5
- Cuisenaire rods or base ten material
- Tape measure or metre rule (optional)

How to play
First player throws the dice and spins the spinner. They complete the appropriate operation (e.g. $4 + 5 = 9$).

They take the correct number of cubes or rods and place them horizontally adjacent to each other so that they form the beginning of a line.

The second player has a turn as above.

(Note: Players should exchange units rods for tens rods when appropriate.)

The winner is the first person to reach 100.

Round 1: Player A throws $5 + 4$ and builds 9 using base ten material

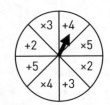

Player A

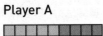

Player B throws 4×5 and builds 20 using base ten material

Player B

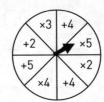

SPIN A STORY

Aims
- To highlight the difference between addition and multiplication.
- To put numbers into contexts.

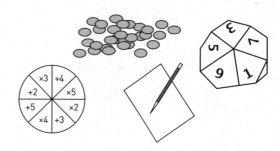

Equipment
- 1 dice 1–10
- 1 spinner × 2, 3, 4, 5 and + 2, 3, 4, 5
- Cubes or counters
- Paper and pencil

How to play
First player throws the dice and spins the spinner.

Write down the number on the dice and the operation on the spinner, e.g. 3 + 4.

Next, take the correct number of cubes or counters to show what this means. Then write the answer.

Example:
3 + 4 =

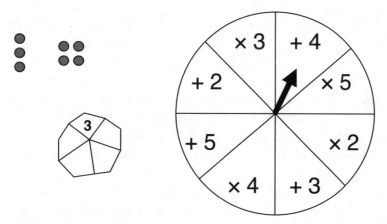

Now make up a story that uses these numbers and the operation.

For example, Centipede's class had 3 green balloons and 4 yellow balloons. How many balloons did they have altogether?

The child draws an illustration for the story.

Appendices

1. Diagnosing Dyscalculia: The Dyscalculia Screener

The Dyscalculia Screener by Professor Brian Butterworth is a computer-based assessment for children aged 6 to 14. The Screener takes into account accuracy and measures response times. The results of the test indicate whether a child is likely to have the specific condition of dyscalculia or whether their difficulties are indicative of low numeracy. Possible factors associated with low numeracy are dyslexia, dyspraxia, attention deficit disorder, maths anxiety or general intelligence levels.

The Dyscalculia Screener tests four areas of number ability:

- simple reaction time
- dot enumeration
- number comparison
- arithmetic achievement.

The **simple reaction time** is calculated by asking the pupil to press a key on the keyboard when a black dot appears on the screen at irregular intervals.

In the **dot enumeration** section the number of dots is sometimes too large to subitize so they would need to be counted in order to achieve accuracy on the task but those with good number sense may perceive groups of dots and so achieve faster time scores than those who count the dots one by one.

In the **number comparison** task the child sees two numbers and is asked which number is 'more'. The smaller number might appear in a larger type size than the greater number. Those with dyscalculic tendencies would be more likely to be slowed down by this effect.

The **arithmetic achievement** tasks involve addition and multiplication. Whether these tasks are included depends on the age of the child.

The results of the Dyscalculia Screener are available immediately in an easily understandable format. A bar chart shows the composite scores on the areas being tested. A short report explains what the scores mean and makes recommendations as to further assessment or intervention. The scores are standardized so that the child's attainment level can be compared with the national average. There is now an online version available with additional features.

2. The Wechsler Intelligence Scale for Children (WISC IV)

How to interpret the WISC IV

This assessment is administered by a chartered psychologist. The psychologist may be a clinical psychologist or an educational psychologist. Generally, the label clinical or educational refers to the type of setting that the psychologist works in, although some clinical psychologists refer to themselves as working in education.

Before assessing children's levels of maths on any assessment, it is helpful to have background information available.

One useful and common way of looking at the strengths and weaknesses that children bring to maths can be understood from their profile shown on The Weschler Intelligence Scale for Children. This is generally known as the WISC and the latest edition is the WISC IV. It is designed to assess children from six years to 16 years 11 months old.

The WISC IV is useful because it not only gives **an overall intelligence score,** where that is possible or appropriate, but also, through the administration of a variety of subtests, it gives information concerning a child's learning strengths and weaknesses. This information not only gives an idea of the child's overall potential but also some indication of what particular teaching style may prove to be successful.

An overall intelligence score can be a useful indicator of future academic success, particularly when no learning difficulties are present. Some variation in overall IQ scores is normal in the general population. However, this overall score can be misleading if there are specific difficulties present, such as dyslexia, dyspraxia or dyscalculia, because there will be an uneven scatter of scores with some subtests showing higher ability and others showing lower ability. In this case, an overall score could be extremely misleading and a little like finding the average of a high number and a low number, where the average found would give little indication of the range of scores used to find that average.

Overall intelligence scores

Overall scores generally range from 40 to 160 with 100 representing an average score.

Ninety-five per cent of children score between 70 and 130. Two-thirds of children score between 85 and 115. Any given IQ figure should be interpreted as that figure plus or minus five. Of course, it must be noted how the child responded to the test and if they were attentive and cooperative, but generally the results should be used as a guide to the child's potential as well as strengths and weaknesses, rather than a definitive score that is set in stone.

The overall score obtained can be classified according to the following:

IQ	Classification	Percentage of children
130+	Very Superior	2.2%
120–129	Superior	6.7%
110–119	High Average	16.1%
90–109	Average	50%
80–89	Low Average	16.7%
70–79	Borderline	6.7%
69 and below	Extremely Low	2.2%

For children with a set of scores which are uneven or 'spiky' when drawn on a graph it can be more useful to consider the four-factor or index scores.

1. The Verbal Comprehension Index (VCI)
2. The Perceptual Reasoning Index (PRI)
3. The Working Memory Index (WMI)
4. The Processing Speed Index (PSI)

Each index is formulated by the scores on the various subtests as follows.

The Verbal Comprehension Index

This index investigates how the child understands and uses oral language. This is the factor that is generally related to educational potential and achievement and is a reasonable predictor of academic success.

Similarities Subtest

The Similarities Subtest is one of the most useful subtest scores to examine because it is essentially looking at the child's ability to think and reason logically using words.

Pairs of words are presented orally and the child is asked to explain the similarity between the objects or concepts.

If maths teaching is going to involve a reasoning-based approach, this subtest may provide some insight into how a particular individual might respond to this approach: the better the score, the better the indication that the child can reason. However, if the child is dyscalculic or has particular difficulties in maths they may not be able to reason as well in maths and about numbers as they can about other verbal material.

Vocabulary Subtest

Words are presented orally to the child and they are asked to explain what they mean.

If a child has poor vocabulary in general, they are less likely to acquire the particular language of maths easily. They may need particular emphasis to be placed on acquiring the language and vocabulary of maths. If the child has acquired a wide vocabulary, this may give an indication that the child will be able to acquire mathematical vocabulary. However, vocabulary acquisition is linked to the facility to understand what the words represent. If there is a particular problem with understanding maths concepts this may impair the ability to acquire the vocabulary associated with that concept.

Comprehension Subtest

Questions are presented orally that require the child to solve everyday problems or to show understanding of social rules and concepts. It also involves knowledge of conventional standards of behaviour, social judgement and maturity, and common sense.

The results on this subtest may affect the child's ability to apply common sense to word problems involved in maths lessons. For example, if a child is not aware of energy-saving practices, so is not sure why lights are turned off when someone leaves a room for a prolonged period, they may have difficulty solving a maths word problem involving time and energy conservation issues. The comprehension subtest looks at logical reasoning using words and as such will give a significant indication of how the child might reason about maths involving words. Even non-verbal maths, such as is found, for example, in non-verbal reasoning involving shapes, will involve thinking about the problem presented using words, so this subtest will also give an indication about the child's ability to use logical thinking when presented with problems in the maths lesson.

Supplementary tests

Information Subtest The student is asked about their general knowledge of common events, objects, places and people. It is designed to measure a child's ability to acquire, retain and retrieve general factual knowledge.

This subtest may give an indication of how much maths-specific knowledge a child is likely to have acquired and retained. If maths problems involve commonly known data such as months of the year or seasons it may be that a child who is weak on general knowledge involving common sequences, such as these, may have particular difficulty when these are included in maths lessons. For example, a child with poor general knowledge may not know how many days there are in certain months.

Word Reasoning Subtest The child is asked to identify common concepts being described in a series of clues. This subtest seems to be rarely used in practice.

This subtest could give further indications of a child's ability to develop mathematical concepts and the ability to add these to existing concepts and to develop new ones. The dyscalculic child may have particular difficulty grasping newly presented mathematical concepts and this subtest could predict their learning aptitude where teaching focuses on concepts as well as facts.

The Perceptual Reasoning Index

This index investigates visuo-spatial and perceptual skills and tests are timed. The child needs to adopt logical strategies to do well.

Block Design Subtest

The child has to build a series of two-dimensional blocks using cubes involving two colours. It is designed to measure the ability to analyse and synthesize abstract visual stimuli. It also involves non-verbal concept formation, visual perception and organization simultaneously processing visual motor coordination, learning and the ability to separate figure and ground in visual stimuli.

Difficulties with this subtest could suggest that the child may find certain aspects of maths difficult, especially lessons involving shapes and visual patterns. They may have difficulties analysing shapes and this might lead to difficulties with topics such as finding areas and perimeters of shapes.

Picture Concepts Subtest

The child is presented with two or three rows of pictures and chooses one picture from each row to form a group with common characteristics.

In maths lessons, weaknesses in this area mean that children may have difficulties with work involving shapes with similar and different characteristics. A low score in this subtest could indicate weak spatial awareness and could affect aspects of the maths lesson such as working with nets of shapes such as cubes, when the child has to visualize how to make a cube from a flat piece of card.

Matrix Reasoning Subtest

The child is asked to look at an incomplete pattern or matrix and select the missing portion from five given options.

Matrix reasoning tasks are considered to be culturally fair and language free, and so are useful for assessing the general intelligence of those who are from different cultures and may not have English as a first language. Items are designed to measure visual information processing, and abstract reasoning skills.

This kind of reasoning may be directly involved in a child's approach to maths problems. If they are able to return to first principles to solve the problem, this may mean that they are able to approach a wide variety of problems which are general and unspecified, involving addition or subtraction for example, and attempt to solve them by applying their on-the-spot reasoning abilities to solve problems independently. This subtest is also designed to measure the child's ability to deal with visually presented information, which will give an indication of how the child might approach more visually oriented tasks in maths.

Supplementary Test: Picture Completion Subtest

The child is asked to identify a missing part from a series of pictures of common objects and scenes. This subtest is designed to measure visual perception and organization, concentration and visual recognition of essential details of objects.

This subtest is also designed to measure logical reasoning and may reflect a child's ability to check their work on paper and notice errors they have made in the process.

The Working Memory Index

Digit Span Subtest

The child is asked to repeat number sequences, which increase in length, forwards and backwards. This subtest measures auditory short-term memory, sequencing skills, attention and concentration. The tasks involve repeating forward sequences, rote learning and memory, attention encoding and auditory processing. The backwards tasks involve working memory, transforming information, mental manipulation and visuo-spatial imaging. The shift between the forwards tasks and the backwards tasks require cognitive flexibility and mental alertness. The forwards task tends to reflect short-term memory for something just heard, whereas the backwards task involves holding what has been heard in mind while manipulating the information to produce the digits heard in reverse order, a task which involves working memory.

Auditory memory is a crucial factor in mathematics learning. When solving a mental maths problem in particular, it is necessary to hold the question in mind while calculating the answer. If the calculation involves more than one step, or if too much time elapses between the question and the answer, the working memory may not be able to keep everything needed in mind for long enough to reach an answer. Children with weak working memories usually find counting backwards and calculating hard because they lose track in the middle of the process. Weakness in counting backwards may suggest a future difficulty in maths lessons with counting backwards in ones or step-counting backwards in groups of numbers such as fives.

Letter–Number Sequencing Subtest

The child is asked to repeat an orally presented sequence of letters and numbers with the numbers getting bigger and the letters in alphabetical order. This subtest involves sequencing, mental manipulation, attention, short-term auditory memory, visuo-spatial imaging and processing speed.

This subtest also involves memory and a weak result may mean the child has difficulty retaining the question in their mind while they calculate or reason to find the answer. Their score on this subtest may be different from the Digit Span Subtest which involves only remembering sequences of numbers. It may be more demanding to have to remember not only numbers but also letters, especially when switching from one category, numbers, to another, the alphabet.

Supplementary Test: Arithmetic Subtest

The child has to mentally solve a series of arithmetic problems and give oral answers. The subtest is timed and involves mental manipulation, concentration, attention, short- and long-term memory, numerical reasoning ability and mental alertness. It may also involve sequencing, fluid reasoning and also logical reasoning.

This subtest will obviously reflect some aspects of the child's mathematical abilities. If the child has to manipulate mathematical information in their mind, this will involve holding that information in mind. Success with this is clearly influenced by the child's memory capacity. The child's reasoning ability with numbers will give indications of their potential to benefit from a reasoning-based, logic-driven approach to maths.

The Processing Speed Index

Coding Subtest

This involves a series of numbers which are each paired with a simple symbol. The child draws the symbol under each corresponding number. This timed subtest measures processing speed but also short-term memory, learning ability, visual perception, visuo-motor coordination, cognitive flexibility, attention and motivation. It may also involve visual and sequential processing.

The visual perception and memory capacity of the child suggested by this subtest result may indicate the potential for being able to utilize visual materials to establish visual cognitive models in their mind that can be used when concrete equipment is not present.

Symbol Search Subtest

The child is shown a series of paired groups of symbols and asked to scan the two groups and say if a target symbol can be seen.

As well as processing speed, this subtest involves short-term visual memory, visual motor coordination, cognitive flexibility, visual discrimination and concentration. It may also involve auditory comprehension, perceptual organization and planning and learning ability.

Short-term visual memory may be involved in copying maths from a board or textbook and a weak result may mean the child may find this kind of task difficult in the classroom.

Supplementary Test: Cancellation Subtest

This is a processing-speed subtest. The child has to scan a random array and a structured arrangement of pictures.

This subtest may give some indication of how the child may scan mathematical material in a textbook. A poor result may mean the child finds it hard to scan a full page of numerals and work out what to do in a textbook.

Conclusions

The educational psychologist who has carried out the assessment will have provided some explanations and comments concerning the results. If a teacher wishes to contact the psychologist, with the permission of the parents, to ask more specifically about the impact of the strengths and weaknesses on mathematical performance and learning, they will usually find that the psychologist welcomes questions and may be able to give further insights into the results.

The teacher will then be able to use the information to plan how to help the child. The plan may involve using, or should involve, the child's strengths in work designed to raise their levels of achievement in maths. Information about the child's weaknesses may help to prepare some aspects of extra help to work on the child's weak areas of processing and learning.

For example, if the child has strong auditory processing and a high verbal intelligence this can be harnessed by working on maths through a reasoning approach, where the child is encouraged to use language to think about what they are doing in maths lessons.

The child who is a visual learner with high non-verbal intelligence may benefit from a more visual approach to maths. This approach is described clearly in Clausen-May's (2005) book, *Teaching Maths to Pupils with Different Learning Styles.*

In this way, the information provided by the WISC assessment can help the teacher to adapt and select a teaching approach that suits the child, while also bearing in mind the child's weak areas of processing and memory. In this way a more successful intervention result may be obtained by being more fully informed about the cognitive profile that the child brings to the maths lesson.

3. The Dyscalculia Assessment

Sample Report

Name of Child: . . . . A. CHILD
Date of birth: . . . .
Age at Assessment: . . . . 10 years and 6 months
Date of Assessment: . . . .
Name of parent/guardian: . . . .
Address: . . . .
Telephone Number: . . . .
Email: . . . .

Maths Assessment

A is a relaxed outgoing child with a mature personality. He did not appear defensive or nervous when we met for the first time. His behaviour was totally appropriate and helpful. He is reported to have no other specific learning difficulties such as dyslexia. Evidence of dyscalculia was found when A was screened on the Butterworth Dyscalculia Screener in [month, year].

His simple reaction time on the screener was unusually slow but certainly the informal assessment in maths confirmed that he has many signs of dyscalculia so I would confirm that the result is highly likely to be accurate, with A performing as a classic dyscalculic in maths. It has been recommended in this informal assessment that A is assessed by a qualified chartered educational psychologist to ensure that his learning strengths and weaknesses are taken into account for any extra help he is given. In this way other learning issues can be evaluated if identified. It is reported by his mother that A has no particular difficulties at school apart from with maths. Pure dyscalculia is relatively rare but does certainly exist in a significant percentage of the population. Current research is only at the beginning of understanding this condition more fully.

Counting

A's estimation skills for small amounts of items are reasonable. He estimated 10 for 9 items which was excellent. He guessed 28 for 23 which was also a very reasonable estimate.

A can count in ones very effectively and this is the main strategy he uses in most maths calculation. He is not fully sure of the structure of the entire number system and was a little unsure of what 10 more than 190 was, although he did tentatively suggest the correct answer, but without any certainty. **Crossing decade boundaries should be checked for counting in ones, fives, tens and hundreds.**

Reading and writing numbers

A was able to write up to 4 digits correctly but became confused when zeros were involved. He read 9,040 as nine thousand and four. This is quite typical of children with dyscalculia. He was able to read up to 5 digits correctly, sometimes with success with zeros. **A needs further place-value work with larger numbers and targeting those involving zeros. A was able to write numbers with 5 digits correctly such as 10,908.**

Doubles, e.g. 2 + 2

A knows easy doubles off by heart but uses his fingers to count the higher doubles in ones only, e.g. 7 + 7. He uses no other strategy, such as bridging to make ten, on this task.

A seemed to understand that if 8 + 8 is 16 then 8 + 9 would be 'just one more': 17. **This shows signs of some reasoning potential involving numbers and could be developed further.**

Dice patterns

A was able to produce the dice patterns from memory up to 6. When thinking of the dice pattern of 6, A was able to perform simple calculations without using his fingers, e.g. $6 = 3 + 3$ so $6 - 3 = 3$. **The work with dice patterns should be extended to patterns up to 10 to develop this reasoning strategy further through the decades.**

Component work

A was able to give various components of 8 such as $7 + 1$, $5 + 3$. He suggested 8 is made from $7 + 2$, showing the need for more work in this area. A used his fingers for calculations involving components and could not see the connection between $8 - 2 = 6$, and $38 - 2 = 36$. He is not seeing connections in this way and does not use basic knowledge to derive more complex answers through the decades. He resorts to his preferred strategy of counting up or down in ones. A used his fingers accurately for all calculations given such as $43 + 7$ and $67 + 3$, although he did have some knowledge of the components of 10.

For adding tens A counts in tens effectively but again without taking advantage of component facts for 100, e.g. $70 + 30$ was step-counted in tens with some checking with fingers.

He needs to study the components of the counting numbers up to 10 and learn to apply and extend the knowledge through the decades for more complex calculations.

Place value

A has little idea of how he could use place-value knowledge for adding single digits to 10. He uses his fingers and counts on for $10 + 7$ and $10 + 4$. He also counted on in ones for $20 + 7$ and $40 + 8$ and also $36 - 6$.

A shows his lack of place-value knowledge when the following errors are observed:

$20 + 100 = 300$
$20 + 1000 = 3000$

However, A did understand $500 - 100 = 400$ and $500 - 10 = 490$. This particular last example was surprising and not characteristic of the maths seen in this assessment. In fact his mother was surprised at this item of success. It does perhaps show that A's knowledge of the number system is developing, albeit slowly. **A would benefit from working on a place-value mat to develop his understanding of the advantages of using place-value knowledge in basic calculations involving adding or subtracting units to 10s numbers.**

Number lines

When A was asked to calculate $53 - 5$ he predictably, given his previous strategies, counted back in ones. An empty number line was given and A began to draw jumps back in ones.

A would be helped if he learnt to use number lines to calculate in appropriate 'chunks' forwards and backwards to increase his efficiency and speed. He should be taught the complementary addition method, to enable him to calculate subtractions by finding the difference between two numbers by counting up rather than back.

Formal column arithmetic

A finds horizontally presented 'mental maths' quite hard, and prefers to record it in columns. He showed he was able to subtract effectively using this formal method involving decomposition or 'borrowing'. The calculation was $73 - 67$ and his answer was correct.

As a fallback position, A showed evidence of being able to 'follow a recipe to survive' and this need not be discouraged.

Adding numbers with answers over 10

A counts in ones and shows no sign of bridging strategies for 8 + 4 and 37 + 5.

He needs to be explicitly taught the bridging strategy for these calculations.

Tables

A has made a reasonable start with his tables and is conceptually aware that tables consist of counting in groups of a certain quantity. He can step-count in 4s, for example, to reach answers in the 4 times table.

He has managed to learn some of his tables by rote and could demonstrate the difference between 2×3 and 3×2 using glass nuggets. He seemed to be more aware of the sharing method to create groups rather than the grouping method which leads more easily to division facts.

A has begun to understand that division is 'your tables backwards'. He meant that the tables' facts give you the division facts with the same numbers involved. So if $4 \times 8 = 32$ then there are eight 4s in 32 and four 8s in 32, for example.

A is still very vulnerable in this area and would benefit from a checking method. He thought that 4×8 were 36.

A would benefit from a universal strategy for tables. If he knew $10 \times 8 = 80$ and therefore $5 \times 8 = 40$ (by the halving concept) he could work out that 4×8 would be 8 less than 40, for example.

Word problems

A was able to solve a simple word problem and explain his answer as a number sentence: 40 boys came for school lunch. There were 10 boys at each table. How many tables were full?

40 divided by 10 = 4 tables.

A would benefit from further work using word problems to underpin his knowledge in all the four basic maths operations but he has shown he is capable of using maths for basic reasoning tasks.

Conclusions

A presents as typically dyscalculic with a poor sense of number; a preferred strategy is often counting in ones. He has a unitary concept of numbers and is relatively unaware of patterns of sequences or patterns within numbers. He does not use efficient strategies. It is not clear if he does not remember strategies or does not understand the strategies he must have been shown. He is not able to invent his own strategies easily.

He has some rote knowledge but is not able to use the knowledge he does have to derive new facts or to reason with extended examples using larger numbers.

A is in urgent need of a specialist maths programme designed for dyscalculics. This should be delivered by a fully trained person on a regular basis. In order to achieve progress A will need to revise his current maths work regularly every day using a cumulative revision programme to keep new work in mind so that it enters long-term memory. A has been referred to R for specialist dyscalculic help.

4. The Dyscalculia Assessment

Summary Maths Profile

Name ....   Date of birth ....

Date of assessment ....   Age at assessment ....

NUMBER SENSE AND COUNTING

Subitizing ☐

Estimating
up to 10 ☐
more than 10 ☐

Counting
forwards in 1s ☐
in 10s ☐
in 5s ☐
in 2s ☐
backwards in 1s ☐
in 10s ☐
in 5s ☐
in 2s ☐

Reading
two-digit numbers (TU) ☐
larger numbers ☐

Writing
two-digit numbers (TU) ☐
larger numbers ☐

CALCULATION

Addition +1, +2
one more +1 ☐
two more +2 ☐

Subtract −1, −2
one less −1 ☐
two less −2 ☐

Dot patterns 1–6 ☐

Doubles
up to 10 ☐
up to 20 ☐

Near doubles
up to 10 ☐
up to 20 ☐

Bonds of ten
addition ☐
subtraction ☐

Number bonds 1–9
addition ☐
subtraction ☐

Bonds of tens
addition (e.g. 47 + ? = 50) ☐
subtraction (e.g. 70 − 6 = ?) ☐

Bonds of 100
addition (e.g. 30 + ? = 100) ☐
subtraction (e.g. 100 − 80 = ?) ☐

PLACE VALUE

Principle of exchange ☐

10 plus a single digit/Tens plus
10 + n ☐
tens plus n (e.g. 20 + n) ☐

Partitioning ☐

Bridging
units + units (e.g. 8 + 5) ☐
tens + units (e.g. 34 + 7) ☐

Unit subtraction
same units subtraction
(e.g. 36 − 6) ☐

Addition +10
ten more ☐

Subtraction −10
minus ten ☐

Subtraction strategies
doubles ☐
bridging back ☐
counting on (shopkeeper's method) ☐

MULTIPLICATION AND DIVISION

Multiplication
Key tables:
×5 ☐   ×10 ☐

Other tables:
×2 ☐   ×4 ☐   ×6 ☐   ×8 ☐
×3 ☐   ×7 ☐   ×9 ☐

demonstration of meaning ☐

Division
grouping concept ☐
sharing concept ☐

WORD PROBLEMS

addition ☐
subtraction ☐
multiplication ☐
division ☐

FORMAL WRITTEN NUMERACY

addition ☐
subtraction ☐
multiplication ☐
long multiplication ☐
short division ☐

5. Group Grid

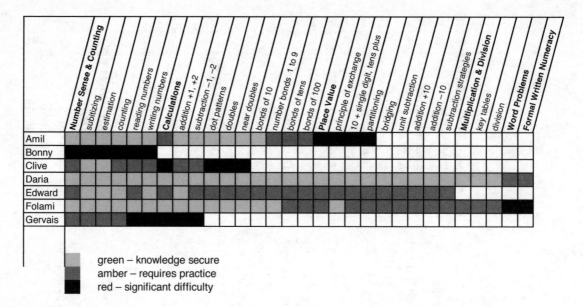

green – knowledge secure
amber – requires practice
red – significant difficulty

Create a spreadsheet for an 'at-a-glance' summary of the knowledge of each child in the class. Enter the data from the Summary Maths Profile for each child to create a spreadsheet using a traffic-light system to colour code the information.

1. Use the Excel spreadsheet.
2. Highlight row 1.
3. Set Font Size at a small point size. Arial 8 gives a clear result.
4. Set Row Height at 80 pixels.
5. Highlight Column A. Set Column Width at 10.
6. Highlight 30 columns (B to AB) and set Column Width at 3.
7. Go to FORMAT → CELLS → ALIGNMENT → ORIENTATION.
8. Set Orientation at 75 degrees either by using the Up arrow or clicking on the Text scale.
9. Start in row 1 column B. Enter each of the topic headings and subheadings in a separate column, e.g. Number Sense and Counting (col. B), Subitizing (col. C), Estimating (col. D), Counting (col. E), etc. The words will appear horizontally but be angled as soon as you finish typing and move to the next cell.
10. Enter the name of each child in column A.
11. Colour code the information. Click on box you want to highlight.
12. Go to FILL COLOUR icon (the bucket) and click on the colour you want (red, amber or green). The box will fill automatically.
13. Colour code the information as follows:
    - Red (black): unable to do this
    - Amber (dark grey): improving
    - Green (light grey): secure knowledge
    - White: not tested because child had made more than two errors on previous section.
14. Finally create borders to all the cells. Highlight all the cells that contain information.
15. Go to the Borders icon on the toolbar and click on the All Borders icon.
16. SAVE DOCUMENT.
17. To print the table highlight everything you want to print.
18. Go to FILE → PRINT AREA → SET PRINT AREA.
19. Print.

6. The Dyscalculia Assessment
Questionnaire for Teachers and Parents

(This form can be filled in by parents, teachers, teaching assistants or others involved with the child concerning their numeracy development.)

Name of child . . . .
Date of birth and present age . . . .
School year group . . . .
Parents' names . . . .
. . . .
Contact details: phone numbers . . . .
and emails . . . .
Teachers' names: . . . .
Contact details: phone numbers . . . .
and emails . . . .

A. **Preschool/nursery-stage number development**
Did the child develop early counting skills applied to stairs or groups of toys? . . . .
Was their counting accurate, touching and counting items one by one? . . . .
Did they remember the names of the numbers easily? . . . .
Did they learn the words of nursery rhymes easily? . . . .
Do they know the days of the week and the months of the year? . . . .
Do they know what year it is now? . . . .

B. **Starting school**
Did the child use their fingers for counting and persist in using their fingers longer than their peers?
. . . .
Did they show any difficulties with numbers at an early stage, writing digits reversed, or confusing numbers like 13 and 31? . . . .

C. **Did their numeracy develop more slowly than their peers?**
. . . .

D. **What is their attitude to maths in school?**
. . . .

E. **What is their attitude to maths given for homework? Do they like doing number work?**
. . . .
. . . .

F. **Do you notice anything unusual about their maths development and are you concerned about it?**
. . . .

G. **Are there any test results available from the school or elsewhere?**
If yes, give details . . . .
. . . .

H. **Has the child had any extra help with maths in school or outside school? If so, did this help and was any progress noted?**
. . . .
. . . .

7. Individual Teaching Plan

Name . . . .

Year . . . .

Date of birth . . . .

Date	Target and criteria for success	Provision	Problems arising	Progress towards target

For extra forms go to: http://education.emersonbabtie.continuumbooks.com

8. Resources

Useful websites

Anna Wilson, University of Canterbury, New Zealand

www.aboutdyscalculia.org

A public information website which is designed to bring scientific information about dyscalculia to parents, teachers and policy-makers.

Brian Butterworth, University College, London

www.mathematicalbrain.com

Updates on the latest research into dyscalculia, and links to resources.

Cambridge University

www.nrich.maths.org/public

Free enrichment material (problems, articles and games) at all key stages for mathematics.

Department for Education

www.education.gov.uk

Getting to Grips with Assessing Pupils' Progress (DfCSF 2008). A pamphlet created by the DCSF containing a three-step guide to assessing pupils' progress (APP) and guidance on using APP to benefit pupils.

www.nationalstrategies.standards.dcsf.gov.uk/node/160703

Diana Laurillard and Hassan Baajour, London Knowledge Lab

www.low-numeracy.ning.com

'Developing Number Sense'. Free prototypes of interactive numeracy games with a forum for discussion. This is part of a Becta-funded research project into 'digital interventions for dyscalculia and low numeracy'.

Dynamo Maths

www.dynamomaths.co.uk

Interactive computer activities for learning and practising basic maths. Based on multi-sensory teaching methods.

dysTalk

www.dystalk.com

Discussion forum for parents and professionals to discuss issues related to dyslexia, dyspraxia and dyscalculia. Interviews with professionals in the field and lists of resources.

Handwriting Without Tears

www.hwtears.com

Comprehensive handwriting programme developed by an occupational therapist.

Keith Holland & Associates

www.keithholland.co.uk

Eyecare services specializing in the treatment of children with learning difficulties.

Learning Works (an educational consultancy)

www.dyscalculia-maths-difficulties.org.uk

A forum for discussing dyscalculia and maths learning difficulties.

Mahesh Sharma, Cambridge College, Massachusetts, USA

www.berkshiremathematics.com

www.bbc.co.uk/skillswise/tutors/expertcolumn/dyscalculia/index.shtml

Article: 'Dyscalculia'.

Stanislas Dehaene, INSERM U562, Paris
www.unicog.org (see the 'Numbers' page)
Updates on the latest research and lists of further academic articles to read.

Equipment suppliers

Counters: glass nuggets
Available from florists and decorative arts suppliers.
Online from:

Emporium Sales & Marketing Ltd
Dicken Green Mill
Greenfield Lane
Rochdale OL11 2LD
Tel: 01706 526548 or 657864
www.emporiumuk.biz/Decorative/Glass_Nuggets.htm

Cuisenaire rods
Educational Solutions (UK) Limited
Unit 5, Feidr Castell Business Park
Fishguard
Pembrokeshire SA65 9BB
Tel: 08456 122912 Fax: 08456 123912
www.cuisenaire.co.uk
(Mini set contains 126 rods; International set contains 310 rods.)

Base ten place-value material (also called Dienes equipment)
Taskmaster Ltd
Morris Road
Leicester LE2 6BR
Tel: 0116 270 4286 Fax: 0116 270 6992
www.taskmasteronline.co.uk

LDA (Learning Development Aids)
Pintail Close
Victoria Business Park
Nottingham NG4 2SG
Tel: 0845 1204776 Fax: 0800 783 8648
www.ldalearning.com

Stern blocks and Stern dual board
Maths Extra Limited
3 North Street
Mere
Wiltshire BA12 6HH
Tel: 01747 861503 Vikki Horner
01444 400601
(Vikki Horner runs training sessions on how to use the
   Stern blocks.)
www.mathsextra.com

Stickers

Stickers are available from high street shops. For bulk purchases try:

Superstickers
PO Box 55
4 Balloo Avenue
Bangor
Co Down
Northern Ireland BT19 7PJ
www.superstickers.com

Transparent spinners

Crossbow Educational
41 Sawpit Lane
Brocton
Stafford ST17 0TE
Tel: 0845 269 7272 or 0845 269 7373
www.crossboweducation.com
(Crossbow is run by Bob Hext, a former special needs teacher.)

Ten-sided dice

Crossbow (see above)
Taskmaster (see above)
LDA (see above)

Useful organizations

Attention Deficit Disorder Information and Support Service (ADDISS)
112 Station Road
Edgware
HA8 7BJ
Tel: 020 8952 2800
www.addiss.co.uk
ADDISS provides information about attention deficit hyperactivity disorder to anyone who needs assistance: parents, sufferers, teachers or health professionals.

The British Dyslexia Association (BDA)
Unit 8 Bracknell Beeches
Old Bracknell Lane
Bracknell RG12 7BW
www.bdadyslexia.org.uk
Tel: 0845 251 9003
National Helpline: 0845 251 9002
The BDA campaigns for a dyslexia-friendly society. It offers support and advice through a network of local Dyslexia Societies and has a network of volunteer befrienders.

Contact a Family

209-211 City Road

London EC1V 1JN

Tel: 020 7608 8700

Helpline: 0808 808 3555

Textphone: 0808 808 3556

www.cafamily.org.uk

Contact a Family provides a range of fact sheets and has a network of volunteer representatives to help families with disabled or special needs children.

CReSTeD

Greygarth

Littleworth

Winchcombe

Cheltenham

Gloucestershire

GL54 5BT

Tel: 01242 604852

www.crested.org.uk

CReSTeD (The Council for the Registration of Schools Teaching Dyslexic Pupils) helps parents, and those who advise them, to choose schools for dyslexic children. All schools included in the Register are visited regularly.

Dyslexia Action

Park House

Wick Road

Egham

Surrey TW20 0HH

Tel: 01784 222300

www.dyslexiaaction.org.uk

Dyslexia Action is the UK's leading provider of services and support for people with dyslexia and literacy difficulties. Dyslexia Action provides assessment, education and training.

Dyslexia Teaching Centre

23 Kensington Square

London W8 5HN

Tel: 020 7361 4790

Fax: 020 7938 4816

www.dyslexiateachingcentre.co.uk

Dyslexia Teaching Centre provides assessment and teaching tailored to individual needs. It offers a range of therapies to people of all ages.

Dyspraxia Foundation

8 West Alley

Hitchin

Herts SG5 1EG

Tel: 01462 454986

www.dyspraxiafoundation.org.uk

The Dyspraxia Foundation offers support and resources to dyspraxics and their families.

Emerson House

40 Redmore Road

Hammersmith

London W6 0HZ

Tel: 020 8741 4554

www.emersonhouse.co.uk

Emerson House is a specialist centre for children aged 5 to 11. It offers assessment and teaching for dyscalculia, dyslexia and dyspraxia.

I CAN

8 Wakley Street

London

EC1Y 7QE

Tel: 0845 225 4071 or 020 7843 2510

www.ican.org.uk

I CAN is an educational charity for children with speech and language difficulties. It provides training and information for parents, teachers and therapists. It runs special schools and nurseries and centres within local schools.

NASEN

Nasen House

4/5 Amber Business Village

Amber Close

Farmington

Tamworth

Staffordshire B77 4RP

Tel: 01827 311500

www.nasen.org.uk

NASEN (National Association for Special Educational Needs) promotes the education, training, advancement and development of all those with special and additional support needs.

Optometrists, speech therapists

British Association of Behavioural Optometrists

21 Hartlebury Way

Charlton Kings

Cheltenham

Gloucestershire GL52 6YB

Tel: 01242 575107

www.babo.co.uk

Behavioural optometrists use lenses and vision training to facilitate the development of a more efficient and complete visual process.

Royal College of Speech and Language Therapists

2 White Hart Yard

London SE1 1NX

Tel: 020 7378 1200

www.rcslt.org

The Royal College of Speech and Language Therapists is the professional body for speech and language therapists and support workers.

Templates

Caterpillar Tracks

Print two copies. Join the sheets leaving a small space between one group of ten and the next.

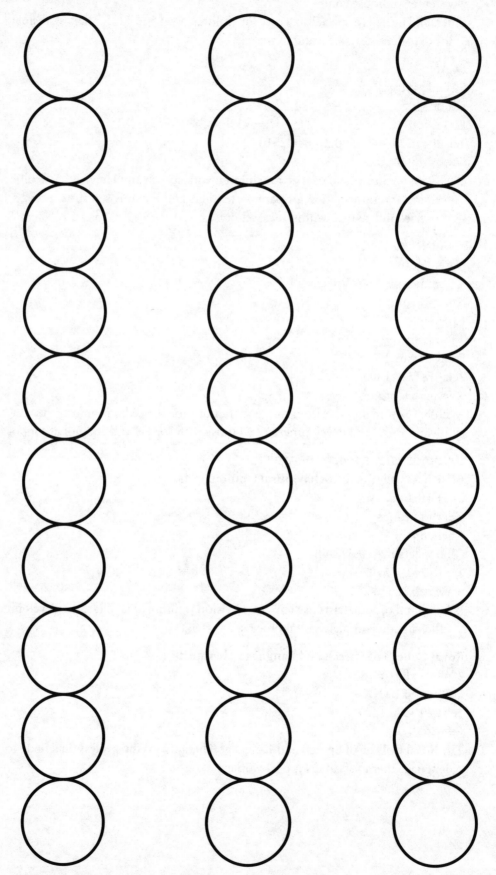

Untangling -teen and -ty

Base sheet

Print one base sheet for each player

-teen	-ty

Untangling -teen and -ty

'-teen' cards

Print one set of '-teen' number cards. Write the suffix '-teen' on the back of each card.

13	14	15	16
17	18	19	
113	114	115	116
117	118	119	

Untangling -teen and -ty

'-ty' cards

Print one set of '-ty' number cards. Write the suffix '-ty' on the back of each card.

20	30	40	50
60	70	80	90
120	130	140	150
160	170	180	190

Pattern Cards 1–10

Four in Order: One set of cards for each player.

Pattern Pairs: One set of pattern cards for a two-player game. Two sets will be required for 3 or more players.

Number Cards 0–10 and Smallest, Largest

Pattern Pairs: One set of numbers 1–10 for a two-player game. Two sets will be required for 3 or more players.

Bonds of Ten Pairs: Two sets of numbers 0–9.

Shut the Box: One set of numers 1–10 (one set for each player).

Clear the Deck: Four sets of numbers 1–9.

Tens and Units Game: Four sets of numbers 0–9 and one each of Smallest and Largest.

			0
1	2	3	4
5	6	7	8
9	10	Smallest	Largest

Word Cards   One–Ten

Pattern Pairs: One set of numbers 1–10 for a two-player game. Two sets will be required for 3 or more players.

		one	two
three	four	five	six
seven	eight	nine	ten

For extra forms go to: http://education.emersonbabtie.continuumbooks.com

Bonds of Ten Pairs

Addition question cards

Print set of question cards plus one set of number cards 0–9.

$1 + \square = 10$	$2 + \square = 10$
$3 + \square = 10$	$4 + \square = 10$
$5 + \square = 10$	$6 + \square = 10$
$7 + \square = 10$	$8 + \square = 10$
$9 + \square = 10$	$10 + \square = 10$

Bonds of Ten Pairs

Subtraction question cards

Print set of question cards plus one set of number cards 0–9.

10 − 1 =	10 − 2 =
10 − 3 =	10 − 4 =
10 − 5 =	10 − 6 =
10 − 7 =	10 − 8 =
10 − 9 =	10 − 10 =

Place-Value Grid
Tens and Units

T	U

Place-Value Grid
Hundreds, Tens and Units

U	
T	
H	

Times Table Cards ×10

Question cards

Print one set of question cards plus one set of answer cards.

Templates for other Times tables available at http://education.emersonbabtie.continuumbooks.com

1 × 10 =	2 × 10 =
3 × 10 =	4 × 10 =
5 × 10 =	6 × 10 =
7 × 10 =	8 × 10 =
9 × 10 =	10 × 10 =

Times Table Cards ×10

Answer cards

Print one set of question cards plus one set of answer cards.

Templates for other Times tables available at http://education.emersonbabtie.continuumbooks.com

		10	20
30	40	50	60
70	80	90	100

Spinner Bases

Games:
Shut the Box
The Multiplication Game
Spin and Track
Spin a Story

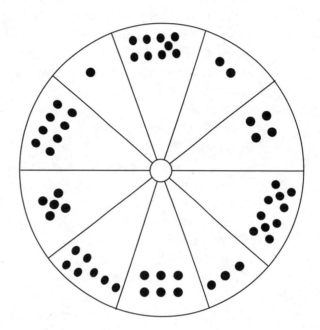

Spinner base for Shut the Box

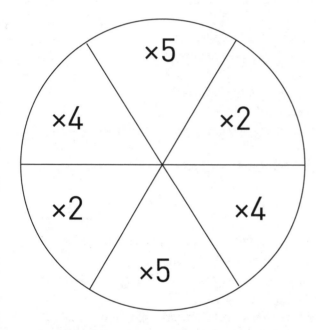

Spinner base for The Multiplication Game

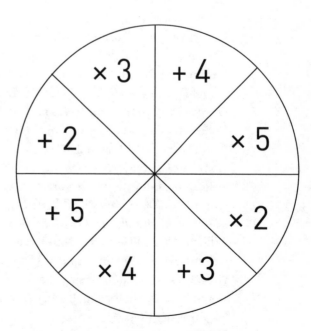

Spinner base for Spin and Track
and Spin a Story

References and further reading

Ashlock, Robert B. (2006), *Error Patterns in Computation: using error patterns to improve instruction*. New Jersey: Pearson Merrill Prentice Hall.

Askew, M. (2004), *BEAM's Big Book of Word Problems* (with *Teachers' Notes*). London: BEAM.

Askew, M., Bibby, T. and Brown, M. (2001), *Raising Attainment in Primary Number Sense: from counting to strategy*. London: BEAM.

Bird, R. (2007), *The Dyscalculia Toolkit: supporting learning difficulties in maths*. London: Paul Chapman.

— (2009), *Overcoming Difficulties with Number*. London: Sage.

Butterworth, B. (1999), *The Mathematical Brain*. London: Macmillan.

— (2003), *Dyscalculia Screener: highlighting children with specific learning difficulties in maths*. London: nferNelson.

Butterworth, B. and Yeo, D. (2004), *Dyscalculia Guidance*. London: nferNelson.

Came, F. and Reid, G. (2007), *CAP It All: a practical manual for assessing individual needs*. Marlborough: Learning Works.

Chinn, S. (2004), *The Trouble with Maths*. Abingdon: RoutledgeFalmer.

Chinn, S. and Ashcroft, R. (1993), *Mathematics for Dyslexics: a teaching handbook*. London: Whurr.

Christmas, J. (2009), *Hands on Dyspraxia: supporting children and young people with sensory and motor learning challenges*. Milton Keynes: Speechmark.

Clausen-May, T. (2005), *Teaching Maths to Pupils with Different Learning Styles*. London: Paul Chapman.

Clayton, P. and Barnes, R. (2004), *How to Develop Numeracy in Children with Dyslexia*. London: LDA.

Dehaene, S. (1997), *The Number Sense: how the mind creates mathematics*. Oxford: Oxford University Press.

Department for Education and Employment (DfEE) (1999), *The National Numeracy Strategy Framework for Teaching Mathematics from Reception to Year 6*. Sudbury: DfEE Publications.

Department for Education and Skills (DfES) (2001), *Guidance to Support Pupils with Dyslexia and Dyscalculia (DfES 0521/2001)*. London: DfES.

Dowker, A. (2004), *What Works for Children with Mathematical Difficulties*. London: DfES Research Report 554. Available online at: www.dcsf.gov.uk/research/data/uploadfiles/RR554.pdf (Accessed 1 March 2009).

Gattegno, C. (1963), *Now Johnny can do Arithmetic: a handbook on the use of colored rods*. Reading: Educational Explorers.

Gifford, S. (2005), *Young Children's Difficulties in Learning Mathematics: review of research in relation to dyscalculia*. QCA/05/1545.

Gillham, W. and Hesse, K. (2001), *Basic Number Screening Test*. London: Hodder.

Grauberg, E. (1998), *Elementary Mathematics and Language Difficulties*. London: Whurr.

Grey, E. (1997), 'Compressing the counting process: developing a flexible interpretation of symbols', in Thompson, I. (ed.) *Teaching and Learning Early Number*. Buckingham: Open University Press.

Hannell, G. (2005), *Dyscalculia: action plans for successful learning in mathematics*. London: David Fulton.

Haylock, D. (2006), *Maths Explained for Primary Teachers*. London: Sage.

Henderson, A. (1998), *Maths for the Dyslexic: a practical guide*. London: David Fulton.

Kay, J. and Yeo, D. (2003), *Dyslexia and Maths*. London: David Fulton.

Kirby, A. (2009), *Dyspraxia: Developmental Co-ordination Disorder.* London: Souvenir Press.

Kosc, L. (1974), 'Developmental dyscalculia'. *Journal of Learning Disabilities,* 7(3), 164–77.

Messenger, C., Emerson, J. and Bird, R. (2007), 'Dyscalculia in Harrow'. *Mathematics Teaching.* 204, 37–9.

Miles, T. R. and Miles, E. (1992). *Dyslexia and Mathematics.* London: Routledge.

Nash-Wortham, M. and Hunt, J. (1997), *Take Time.* Stourbridge: Robinswood Press.

New Jersey Mathematics Coalition (1996), *New Jersey Mathematics Curriculum Framework.* Available online at: http://dimacs.rutgers.edu/nj_math_coalition/framework/acrobat/chap06.pdf (Accessed 30 March 2010).

Rose, J. (2009), *Identifying and Teaching Children and Young People with Dyslexia and Literacy Difficulties.* Available online at: http://publications.dcsf.gov.uk/eOrderingDownload/00659-2009DOM-EN.pdf (Accessed 28 March 2010).

Shalev, R. J., Auerbach, J. *et al.* (2000), 'Developmental dyscalculia:prevalence and prognosis'. *European and child and adolescent psychiatry,* 9(2), 58–64.

Sharma, M. (2003), 'Dyscalculia' DVD. *BBC Skillswise.* Berkshire: Berkshire Mathematics. www.berkshiremathematics.com/video_info.asp

Tapson, F. (2006), *Oxford Mathematics Study Dictionary.* Oxford: Oxford University Press.

Thompson, I. (1997), *Teaching and Learning Early Number.* Buckingham: Open University Press.

——. (1999), *Issues in Teaching Numeracy in Primary Schools.* Buckingham: Open University Press.

Wilson, A. (2004), *Dyscalculia Primer and Resource Guide.* Organisation for Economic Co-operation and Development, Directorate for Education. Available online at: www.oecd.org/document/8/0,3343,en_2649_35845581_34495560_1_1_1_1,00.html (Accessed 23 September 2009).

Yeo, D. (2003), *Dyslexia, Dyspraxia and Mathematics.* London: Whurr.

Glossary

Algorithm: A step-by-step procedure used to perform a calculation.

Area model in multiplication: The multipliers are displayed as unit squares in rows and columns to form a rectangle. The product is the area of the rectangle.

Arithmetic: The branch of mathematics concerned with computation of numbers using the four operations of addition, subtraction, multiplication and division.

Array model: Counters are arranged in rows and columns to create a rectangle where the multipliers are the length of the rows and columns.

Assessment, informal diagnostic: Not timed or standardized, it is conducted in a friendly, relaxed way. The aim is to explore how a child is thinking in order to work out why they are having difficulties and underachieving so that a personalized teaching plan can be developed.

Attention deficit disorder (ADD): Causes inattention and distractibility making it difficult to concentrate. Children with ADD rarely experience pauses in their thoughts, actions or responses to questions and tend to be impulsive. If a degree of hyperactivity is also involved, the condition can be described as attention deficit hyperactivity disorder (ADHD).

Bridging: A strategy that applies bonds of ten knowledge to work out calculations. Ten, or a multiple of 10, is used as a 'stepping stone' to add two numbers where the answer will be more than 10. Example: $5 + 8 = (5 + 5) + 3 = 10 + 3 = 13$.

Bridging back: Using ten or a multiple of ten as a 'stepping stone' to subtract a number calculation. Example: $23 - 5 = (23 - 3) - 2 = 20 - 2 = 18$.

Cardinal number: Denotes the quantity or size of a set of objects. The last number in a count represents the quantity in the group (e.g. 1, 2, 3, 4 so there are 4).

Chunking: Putting numbers or objects together to form a group in a calculation rather than calculating using ones.

Co-morbidity: A condition that occurs at the same time as another condition but is not related to it.

Commutative: Describes an arithmetical operation in which the order of the numbers does not change the outcome. Addition and multiplication are commutative. Example: $2 + 3 = 5$ and $3 + 2 = 5$ or $7 \times 8 = 56$ and $8 \times 7 = 56$. Subtraction and division are not commutative.

Complement of a number: The number that is added to another number to complete a specified quantity. Example: If the specified quantity is 10 and you have 2, the complement of 2 will be 8.

Complementary addition: The difference between two numbers is found by counting on from the smaller number up to the larger number in ones or in groups. (Also known as the 'shopkeeper's method'.) Example: $73 - 65$: start at 65 and count on in ones until you reach 73. The difference is the number counted on which is 8.

Component number: A constituent part of a specified number. Example: $7 = 4 + 3$ where 3 and 4 are the components of 7.

Counting: Enumerating objects by matching each object to a specific number name in a sequence.

Counting all: Starting counting in ones from the first number in a calculation. If this is used as a calculation strategy it is evidence of very poor number sense.

Counting on: Starting with a number and counting on from that number in ones. Children need this ability but they should develop more efficient calculating strategies over time.

The Counting Trap: Numbers are seen as a collection of ones so each operation is seen as an instruction to count. Number facts never become known automatically and the very counting becomes a 'trap'.

Crossover point: A term used to describe the point in a counting sequence when the name of the tens number changes. For example, in the sequence … 28, 29, 30, 31, 32 … the crossover point is 30 because the tens name changes from **twenty** in twenty-nine to **thirty**.

Decade boundary: In counting, this is the point in the number system at which one group of tens ends and another begins. For example, in the sequence … 28, 29, 30, 31, 32 … the decade boundary falls between 30 and 31. This causes confusion for some children as the 30 is at the end of the twenties decade, not the beginning of the thirties in counting terms. The next decade starts with 31. (Compare this with crossover points.)

Dice patterns: The patterns for the numbers 1 to 6 found on a conventional dice.

Dot patterns: Number patterns to 10 derived from the conventional dice patterns. The dot patterns make the doubles and near doubles facts explicit.

Doubles facts: The number bonds created by doubling a number, also expressed as adding a number to itself. Example: 8 = 4 + 4.

Dyscalculia: Developmental dyscalculia is a condition that affects the ability to acquire arithmetical skills. Dyscalculic learners may have difficulty understanding simple number concepts, lack an intuitive grasp of numbers and have problems learning number facts and procedures. Even if they produce a correct answer or use a correct method, they may do so mechanically and without confidence (DfES 2001).

Dyslexia: "Dyslexia is a learning difficulty that primarily affects the skills involved in accurate and fluent word reading and spelling. Characteristic features of dyslexia are difficulties in phonological awareness, verbal memory and verbal processing speed. Dyslexia occurs across the range of intellectual abilities. It is best thought of as a continuum, not a distinct category, and there are no clear cut-off points. Co-occurring difficulties may be seen in aspects of language, motor co-ordination, mental calculation, concentration and personal organisation, but these are not, by themselves, markers of dyslexia. A good indication of the severity and persistence of dyslexic difficulties can be gained by examining how the individual responds or has responded to well-founded intervention." (Rose 2009)

Dyspraxia: Developmental dyspraxia, also known as developmental coordination disorder (DCD), is characterized by the inability to carry out and plan sequences of coordinated movements to achieve an objective (Kirby 2009).

Enumeration: Finding out how many items there are in a group by synchronizing one number name with each object in the count.

Estimate: The ability to guess roughly how many items there are in a group without counting, or to round numbers in a calculation to give the approximate size of the answer. Estimation is particularly important for successful use of calculators.

Exchange, principle of: A specific number of items can be exchanged for a single item which then represents those initial numbers or quantities, e.g. 10 one pence coins equals 1 ten pence coin, 7 days equals one week.

Finger agnosia: Not knowing where your fingers are in space.

Finger counting: Moving and touching fingers to aid counting. Children need to use their fingers to count initially as this is 'an important precursor to learning base ten' (Dehaene 1997). However, persistent use of fingers to count large quantities of ones often leads to inaccuracies. Finger counting can be used effectively if it is used to keep track of groups of numbers as in multiplication.

Formative assessment: An interactive assessment in which the teacher identifies the difficulties a child is having and uses the information to prepare a teaching plan to assess those difficulties. This approach is also called assessment for learning.

Individual education plan (IEP): Sets out the long-term goals and the short-term targets needed to achieve those goals, as well as detailing the additional teaching or support that will be needed. Now increasingly being superseded by provision maps or School Action Plans.

Key number bonds: Number bonds, or number components, are two numbers that are added together to make another number. The key number bonds are: doubles, near doubles, bonds of ten.

Key number facts: Bonds of ten, doubles and near doubles bonds, and multiplication by 10. Number facts need to be known 'off by heart' as they underpin calculation. Other number facts can be derived from the key facts.

Left–right orientation: Understanding the concept of the relationships between objects in spatial terms and being able to correctly apply the terms left and right to your own orientation and that of other people and objects.

Long-term memory: The ability to store information which can be retrieved again over a reasonably long period of time.

Mantra: A phrase or instruction that is learnt by rote and repeated to help remember facts or carry out calculations. This may be helpful if remembered correctly. However, some can be quite complicated and lead to problems if parts are forgotten or misapplied. Example of a mantra for mental calculation: 'Five in my head [points to head and touches it] and three fingers up [puts hand with three fingers up]'. Says again: 'Five in my head [touches head] six, seven, eight [touches each finger as counts 6, 7, 8]'.

Maths anxiety: Fear of mathematics which creates a psychological barrier, making it difficult, or impossible, for the person affected to solve mathematical problems.

Memory weaknesses: Auditory memory weakness will affect mental maths. Visual memory weakness may cause difficulties working from the board or from textbooks with a busy layout. Memory weaknesses make it difficult to learn new information and to remember it in the long term.

Multi-sensory teaching: Involving all the senses of touch, sight, hearing and speech.

Near doubles facts: The number bonds that are created by adding adjacent numbers. Example: $4 + 3 = 7$.

Number bonds: The fixed relationship between a number and its constituent parts. Usually taught as pairs of numbers which are combined to make another number. Example: $9 = 5 + 4$ which can also be expressed in a variety of ways such as $9 - 4 = 5, 9 - 5 = 4, 5 + 4 = 9$.

Number line: Numbers are marked on a line at regular intervals. Fractions can be shown in the intervals between the whole numbers. Number lines can be a useful aid in calculation; however, children need to understand how the number line relates to the number track. The difference between a number track and a number line is that a number track only shows whole numbers. Fractions as well as whole numbers can be marked on a number line.

Number sense: A 'feel' for numbers which involves understanding that a number represents a specific quantity or value which is part of a sequence and can be compared with other numbers.

Number track: A number track shows whole numbers. Each number occupies a defined space on the track. The easiest way to show the difference between a number track and a number line is to measure unit cubes against a ruler where the cubes are comparable to a number track and the ruler is a number line.

Numerical operations: Addition, subtraction, multiplication and division.

Numerosity: The acquisition of the concept of numerosity means that you can decide whether two collections do or do not contain the same quantity. It also involves the ability to detect a change in quantity.

One-to-one correspondence: Each number word is mapped onto, or associated with, one object in a group being counted.

Ordinal number: Describes the position of a number in a sequence, e.g. first, second, third, fourth.

Partitioning: Breaking a number into constituent parts to make it easier to perform calculations. Numbers can be partitioned in various ways but early on it is best to use the term when partitioning numbers into hundreds, tens and units to reinforce place-value knowledge. Example: $435 + 62 = 400 + 30 + 5 + 60 + 2 = 400 + 90 + 7 = 497$.

Place value: The value of a digit is determined by its position or place in a number. For example, in 635 the 6 represents 6 hundreds (600), the 3 represents 3 tens (30) and the 5 is worth 5 ones or units (5). The place-value pattern of hundreds, tens and units is repeated throughout the number system to build up larger numbers.

Processing speed: How quickly children can take in oral or visual information. If they process the information slowly the pace of lessons in a classroom may be too fast for them so that they cannot understand or remember what has been taught.

Provision map: A chart drawn up by a SENCO showing what help a child is receiving in each area of the curriculum and who is providing the support.

Recitation: Learning the number names and reciting them in sequence.

SENCO: Special Educational Needs Coordinator who is responsible for ensuring that children with special needs have their needs assessed and met through appropriate provision.

Sequences of numbers: An ordered list of numbers that is governed by a rule which defines the relationship between them. The rule might be 'add one' as in the counting sequence 1, 2, 3, 4, 5. Or it might be 'add 5' as in counting in fives.

Shopkeeper's method: See complementary addition.

Short division: Dividing by a single-digit number.

Short-term memory: Recalls things that are only needed temporarily for immediate use, such as remembering a new telephone number. Once the information has been used it can be forgotten without adverse effects.

Step-counting: Counting forwards or backwards in groups. Children should be able to step-count in tens, fives and twos. It is useful but not essential to be able to step-count in threes and fours. Step-counting in higher numbers will probably be too difficult for children with a memory weakness. Example: To calculate 4×5 step count 5, 10, 15, 20.

Subitizing: The ability to take in the quantity of a random array of objects at a glance and without counting.

Subtraction strategies: The subtraction strategies suggested in this book are: doubles subtraction – recognizing number combinations as part of doubles patterns, bridging back through ten, and complementary addition often known as the shopkeeper's method.

Subvocalizing: Talking to yourself under your breath about what you are thinking. Sometimes there is slight lip movement. Subvocalizing is not wrong. Talking through what they are doing is exactly what you want the child to do. However, they should be reasoning to help develop their thinking, not simply repeating information or procedures learnt by rote.

Tally marks: Recording a number of items by writing one symbol, usually a line, for each item in the count. To make it easier to read, four vertical lines are recorded and the fifth is a diagonal that crosses the four. This makes it easy to compute the total tally at the end of the count. Tally marks are efficient for recording data for statistical analysis. However, some children persist in using them to do calculations with large numbers which is inefficient and prone to errors.

Teaching plan: A detailed plan of what to teach and how to teach it, taking into account the child's level of knowledge and style of learning.

Unit subtraction: Subtracting a single digit from a multi-digit number where the number to be subtracted is the same as the unit digit in the larger number.

Universal strategy: A strategy that can be applied in a variety of situations. Example: Bridging through ten can be applied to both addition and subtraction and adapted for larger numbers.

Visual perception: The ability to interpret what you see in a meaningful way.

Visual and spatial awareness: The ability to see the distances between objects and the relationships among them. The child who cannot do this may get lost finding their place on a page and returning to it.

Visualizing: Thinking in pictures or images. If a child is silent and appears to be staring into space they may be seeing still or moving pictures in their head. The ability to retain a mental image to recall when needed plays an important part in memory.

Working memory: The memory needed to carry out step-by-step procedures and to reason.

Zero: The place-value holder that denotes an empty position in a multi-digit number.

Index

abacus 87–8, 98

abstract symbols 3

activities xi, 4, 84–5, 107, 130, 132, 135–8

ADD *see* attention deficit disorder

addition 36–9, 45, 46, 50, 70, 76
    bonds of ten 4, 18, 35, 50–1, 53, 91, 98–9, 104, 130, 133, 136, 158–9
    bridging through ten 16, 18, 55, 104–5, 112
    complementary addition 53, 58–9, 92, 110–11, 163
    counting all 18, 36, 38, 91–3, 96, 102
    counting on 6, 18, 36, 38, 50, 53, 86, 91–2, 96, 99, 102, 104–5, 108–9, 148, 165
    counting in ones 7, 18, 30, 102, 105, 110, 119
    chunking 110
    doubles 18, 35, 42, 92–3
    early calculation +1, +2 36–7, 38–9, 91
    formal written 76, 78, 123–4
    in multi-digit numbers 106, 108–9, 122
    involving exchange 125–6
    missing addend 48, 50, 53, 84, 99
    near doubles 35, 44, 48, 58, 92–6
    number lines 14, 16, 54, 58, 99, 104, 108–12
    repeated 61, 113, 117
    reasoning 4, 12, 14, 16, 42, 88, 92–3, 96
    word problems 69, 70, 121
    see also calculation, dot patterns, number patterns

addition problems 102, 122
    question cards 146, 181
    skills 108–9

ADHD *see* attention deficit hyperactivity disorder

age 14, 140, 156
    reading 83

algorithm 75, 78–80, 123, 125

answer card 146, 153, 185–6

anxiety
    general 20–1, 82, 113, 120
    maths *see* maths anxiety

apparatus 87 *see also* Base Ten material, bead strings, counters, Cuisenaire rods, Slavonic abacus, Stern blocks

approximation 3, 25, 112, 123–4, 127

area model (in multiplication) 61, 69, 113, 117, 118, 122, 128, 138

arithmetic 4, 7, 14, 112, 123, 125, 156, 160, 163
    skills 1

array 4, 114–15, 118, 128, 138, 152, 161
    model (in multiplication) 69, 113, 117–18, 122, 152

Ashlock, R 127

Askew, M 122

assessment 2, 4, 11–14
    computer-based 2, 10, 156
    diagnostic ix, 13
    informal 11, 13, 162
    qualitative 7
    selection for 11

attention deficit disorder (ADD) 2, 7–8, 10, 13

attention deficit hyperactivity disorder (ADHD) 2, 7, 10, 13

attention levels 20

attention span, short 83

attitudes ix, 16, 19–20, 22–3, 82–3, 96

audio recording 10

auditory discrimination 9, 28, 90–1

auditory sequential memory 86–7

automatic knowledge 32–3, 35

automaticity 87, 89, 91

'big-value' strategies 115

base ten 7, 17, 25–6, 84–5, 87–8, 91, 98, 100–2, 106, 108, 124–5, 132, 137, 140, 142, 149–51, 154, 170, 175

base ten equipment 101, 108, 132, 137, 149–50, 170

Basic Number Screening Test 13

bead strings 98–9

billions 103

Index